SCHOLASTIC INC.
New York Toronto London Auckland Sydney
Mexico City New Delhi Hong Kong

Holiday in Your Heart

LeAnn Rimes
and Tom Carter

ISBN 0-439-16260-2

12 11 10 9 8 7 6 5 4 3 2 1   .   9/9 1 2 3 4/0

Printed in the U.S.A.   37

First Scholastic printing, November 1999

Book design by Brian Mulligan.

Although the following story is almost entirely fiction, it makes a point that has always been—and always will be—the truth.

—LeAnn Rimes and Tom Carter

Acknowledgments

This book, like my entire career, would not have been possible without the support of my parents, Wilbur and Belinda Rimes, and my comanager, Lyle Walker. Rod Essig and Sally Willcox at Creative Artists Agency and Sandy Friedman at Rogers & Cowan were essential to the book's promotion. Tom Carter and I communicated like family. The suggestions from Pat Mulcahy, my editor at Doubleday, made for dramatic improvement of this story. I also want to thank Dean Williamson and Al Lowman at Authors and Artists Group for all of their work on the project.

—LeAnn Rimes

Pat Mulcahy is an insightful and imaginative editor who is a writer's dream. She takes his best and makes it better. Invaluable suggestions were also tendered by Sally Willcox of Creative Artists Agency. Dean Williamson, at Authors and Artists Agency, is a literary agent who's the personification of persistence. He helped foster, and then nurtured, this project from start to finish. My associate Rebecca Holden consistently offered fresh and objective ideas. I concur with LeAnn's words regarding her parents, Lyle Walker, Sandy Friedman and Rod Essig. It was an overwhelming delight to work with LeAnn, one of the most creative people I've ever met at any age. I wish people would focus more on her talent and less on her teens.

—Tom Carter

Holiday in Your Heart

Chapter One

MANY LITTLE girls dream of becoming a princess.

My pretend throne wasn't a giant chair surrounded by busy servants with ivory combs. I never imagined a handsome prince on a white horse riding with me into the sunset and happiness forever after.

I'm a singer who dreamed of performing on the Grand Ole Opry. The Nashville music business people call it country music's Carnegie Hall. Somebody said that a country singer making it to the Opry is like a baseball player making it to the World Series, but I think the Opry might be a bigger deal. A baseball player has eight teammates on the field. There is a band and background singers on the Opry, but it's just you out front—standing alone where everybody in country music has stood.

I had stood there a thousand times in my dreams before I stood there in real life.

I used to pretend I was singing on the Opry when I was five years old and first sang in front of people outside of my family. My dad let me sing with his band. He wouldn't play in places that served alcohol because the law wouldn't let me sing there. He gave up a lot of income he could have earned in honky-tonks, just so I could sing with him at the family places. I wonder now how the other band members felt about that.

My dad has perfect pitch, and together we have what some folks call "bloodline harmony." Either of us can sing melody and the other the high part. Our voices fit like gloves.

One of my favorite pastimes is to watch home movies of my dad and me on the bandstands we played around Mississippi and Texas. My head doesn't even come to the bottom of his guitar. My face is thrown up to look at his face, leaning over his guitar, looking down at me. We watched each other's lips and sang every part of every word at exactly the same time. The people loved it.

I had to hold the microphone in my hand because it

was too tall on the stand, even when the stand was lowered as far as it would go.

My favorite memories about Dad and our music come from singing in the car. We sang everywhere he drove, whether we were on the way to a show or the grocery store. Dad drove old cars that always had a hump on the floor of the backseat. I asked what was under the hump and he told me the "singing monster." He said the monster ate little girls who sang off-key. I just giggled. He eventually told me the hump covered the car's driveshaft, whatever that is.

I preferred the monster story.

I remember standing many times with my feet spread over that hump, my arms and chin resting on top of the front seat. Dad drove and we both sang to the windshield. Mom rode in the front passenger's seat and requested songs. We played a game where she put her hands over her ears if she thought she heard a sour note, or if the tempo dragged, or any other mistake.

Near the end of those days, the only place Mom ever put her hands was together—to applaud for Dad and me.

Dad sold oil field supplies for a company where Mom worked as a receptionist. He worked with his hands and sometimes didn't get all the grease off his skin. His soiled fist gripped the steering wheels of our old cars as tightly as a ship's captain. To me, his workingman's hand looked as big as a roast beef with fingers. I can still see his grip shaking with the vibrations of the steering wheel. Our cars always shook because the tires were out of line from Dad's driving into the oil fields. Daddy's grip was strong and sure. To me, he always had those old cars—and his family members' lives—firmly under control.

After our shows, I'd get sleepy and curl up on the floor of the backseat and put a pillow on top of that hump. I could rest secure knowing Dad was at the wheel with Mom by his side. Dad drove through the summer nights with the windows down to save gasoline the air conditioner would have required. The rush of the wind into the car blended with the static from the faraway country music stations in the rural South that Dad tried to get on the radio. I curled into a tighter ball and fell asleep to the wind, static, and hum of the highway speeding under the car. The last words I always heard were from Mom, telling Dad not to talk because he would keep me awake.

I've never felt more safe.

I shared some of those childhood memories with entertainers backstage at the Opry. Many of them talked about the times they visited the Opry as children. Their eyes took on a faraway look as they recalled their first experience there. Most saw their first Opry performance at Nashville's old Ryman Auditorium. That was where the Opry was for thirty-six years before moving to the Grand Ole Opry House in 1974, eight years before I was born. I remember the date because it's written on a gold sign that's so shiny, I used it as a mirror before going on-stage. I wish it had been a real mirror; then I wouldn't have gotten my lipstick higher on one side.

I have a new dream today.

I stopped dreaming about playing the Opry in the fall of 1996 when the dream came true. I walked onto the platform of the seventy-two-year old radio show, the world's longest-running live broadcast. (I found out because the announcer kept saying it.) A cameraman from a television news show was behind me. So were my daddy's pride and my mama's tears.

I took a deep breath and inhaled the smell of the hot dogs in the lobby. A parade of people streamed to the footlights to take my picture. Hundreds took snapshots from their seats. There were so many flashes that it looked like strobe lighting inside the auditorium. Old men and women smiled at me, some through missing teeth, and little children stood in their seats to sing along.

When I was little, my relatives used to tease me and say that my first kiss would be my greatest thrill. They were wrong; playing the Opry was much more sensational. My first kiss gave me a tingle, but only because I cut my lip on the boy's braces.

I've heard grown-ups talk about "sensory overload." That's when you enjoy something so much it seems like it isn't really happening because you can't absorb it all. It must be like sleepwalking through a dream. I think I had sensory overload the first time I played the Grand Ole Opry.

My wish of becoming a princess had come true. My throne was a brick building with a balcony, a high ceiling, and Coca-Cola for sale.

I talked to a lot of the Opry's old performers that night, but not as many as I would have liked. I was at a loss for words when I sat backstage, face-to-face with people whose records I'd listened to for as long as I can remember.

I think the thing I liked most was that the entertainers talked to me. I know they knew I was nervous. All these famous performers who had all these hit songs were asking how they could make me comfortable. Me—the new kid on the block. They had their own dressing rooms, yet many came to mine just to say hello and to walk lightly into my dream.

I returned to Nashville a couple of months later, in November 1996, to play again at the Grand Ole Opry House. I was pleased to be on the program so close to Christmas.

Between shows, my mom and dad and I walked around the giant Opry grounds. I've traveled all over the United States and Canada during my short life. I've been to New York City at Christmastime. But I've never seen anything like Opryland during the winter holidays.

Imagine a hotel with almost five thousand rooms and an electric candle in every window. Imagine spruce trees so tall you have to bend your back to see the top and so heavily covered with lights, you can't even tell they're green. There are hundreds like that on the grounds.

I felt like I was someone in the Bible when I walked through the place that represented the birth of the baby Jesus. There were live camels and men dressed like the three wise men, and they knelt before a manger with a real baby.

I asked my mom why the baby didn't get cold. She asked a security guard, and he said the infant was under an electric blanket on top of hay that was heated. Its real mother was close by, but she wasn't in costume, so everybody thought she was one of the tourists. The guard said they took the baby out of the manger and put in another one about every thirty minutes.

I asked if the babies were paid. The guard said yes, and I wondered if the babies or their mothers got the money. And if the babies got it, who signed their checks?

I felt like Dorothy in *The Wizard of Oz*, except here the wizard was Santa Claus, and there were a hundred tin men, except they were really giant candy canes with human legs. I never figured out how the people inside the canes could see. I also didn't understand why they didn't tip over, since they must have been top-heavy. How could you walk with a striped tube forty feet tall on top of your head while taking baby steps in house shoes made of red-and-white fake fur?

The air was filled with the sound of children laughing. It blended merrily with the Christmas music coming from speakers on almost every tree.

No child could imagine a better Christmas setting. Opryland was for children of all ages.

"I wish Grandma Teeden could see this, Mom," I said. Mom agreed. Whenever we saw nice things, it seemed we always thought about my dad's mother, Grandma Teeden and how much she'd enjoy them.

Her real name is Teresa, but I couldn't pronounce that when I was tiny. So she became my Grandma Teeden.

Grandma Teeden looked like a real-life Aunt Bea on the old *Andy Griffith Show*. She even had a bun, a tight roll of hair that sat firmly on the back of her head. She was short and heavy and unconcerned about both. She pleased herself by pleasing others. That pudgy, lovable woman always had a heart bigger than her waistline.

She believed in hard work with a passion, having grown up on her farm in Leesburg, Mississippi. It wasn't really a farm, just a big house on ten acres with a garden, two cats, and a beagle. But "farm" is what the family always called it.

Anyhow, I was talking about her work habits. When

Grandpa Luther was laid off from a cobbler's shop, he stood in an unemployment line that formed at 9 A.M. But Grandma Teeden demanded that he be out of bed, shaved and dressed by daylight. Then she'd make him sit in front of her front room window until after sunrise, so people going to work could see him through the glass. She wanted her neighbors to know that her man didn't lie in bed. She wanted them to know he was ready to work at looking for work. Anything else in an able-bodied man, she believed, was indecent.

I looked around at the strolling vendors selling Christmas cookies at Opryland and thought of Grandma Teeden. Her house always smelled like gingerbread at Christmastime and like homemade pies the rest of the year. That woman cooked every meal she and Grandpa Luther ate. Meat and potatoes, pie and coffee. She's never had fast food and never ordered a pizza. That's good because there is no pizza place in her little town.

She made plump pies and cakes that were clouds with icing. So whenever I ate baked goods, as I did at Opryland, I couldn't help but compare them to Grandma Teeden's. I think you can guess whose were better.

She made everything from scratch, nothing from a recipe. My mom calls that cooking by feel and has told me it will take years for me to get the knack of it.

Grandma Teeden was my second mom. Her own

daughter had drowned when she fell through the top of a well. Her name was Rachel, and sometimes Grandma Teeden called me that by mistake.

I sometimes spent nights with her. I was afraid to run the short distance between her house and ours in the dark, so she always turned on her porch light and stood where I could see her. I sprinted across the yard and landed with pounding heart into her open arms.

Her faith was as much a part of her life as her marriage. She believed a woman should have one man—and one God—during her life. She sat in the same seat in the same church house three times a week. Everybody in the congregation knew that was Teresa's seat. No one else dared sit in it. A visitor once took that seat, and Grandma Teeden told him the Lord had told her he should move. He didn't stay for the service.

The building had an old wooden floor that was scratched where Grandma Teeden tapped her heels for years, keeping time to the music. The deep scars are there to this day.

When I wasn't singing with my dad, I sang in Grandma Teeden's church. The place had no air-conditioning, and people kept cool with handheld paper fans donated by the local funeral home. I couldn't see over the pulpit, so I stood to its side. I looked straight at Grandma Teeden, who moved her fan back and forth to the tempo of my song. I was supposed to let her movement keep time, instead of tapping my foot. The first time we tried that, it didn't work. I couldn't see her fan, held under her chin. Too many heads were in the way.

So Grandma later held her fan above her head and made her movements wide enough for me to see from the platform. She waved the fan with her arm instead of her wrist. Her raised arm looked like that giant thing that swings on grandfather clocks, turned upside down. She moved enough air to cool her and the people beside her.

I just kept singing.

The preacher once told me he had been in the Navy and was stationed on an aircraft carrier. He said Grandma's motions reminded him of a flight director bringing an airplane onto a deck.

I preferred to think she was signaling the angels and that they were always in our services.

Grandma always tried to hide her laughter at my misbehavior when I was little. She'd fake sternness and tell me when I'd done something wrong. Then she'd quickly turn her back to me and face her kitchen sink. I didn't actually hear her laughing, but I saw it. The bun on the back of her head bounced whenever she giggled over her dishes.

My Grandma Teeden taught me that one only truly loves life when one loves God. I thought about that in the Opryland hoopla. There was just so much love in the nippy holiday air.

"God in your life puts a holiday in your heart," she always said. "You know your soul is in good standing if you feel that holiday in your heart."

And then she'd talk about God as if she were talking about a personal friend. To her, He was.

I don't think anybody can see children at Christmastime without thinking about their own favorite Christmas. Mine came when I was small and was the result of a plot involving my parents, Grandma Teeden, and Grandpa Luther.

This may sound corny, but remember, I was only four. I actually think this is the first thing I remember about my life.

They all decided I should have a live "reindeer."

Grandpa Luther took down some old antlers he had mounted in his barn. Somehow he attached them to the head of a calf—as in baby cow. One of my grandparents somehow taped a red stocking cap over the calf's nose and mouth.

Years later, they explained how they taped the calf's tail to the inside of its leg, cut a white rag into a point, then attached the rag to the top of its tail. The white cloth stood up, much like a deer's tail.

They waited until just before nightfall on Christmas Eve, then told me Rudolph was outside. They figured I wouldn't be able to see clearly because of the darkness and because I'd be afraid to get close to the animal.

They were right.

So I stood there and looked at that pathetic calf. It moved its head quickly, and one set of antlers fell off.

"Is that what Rudolph does before he gets ready to fly?" I asked.

"Oh . . . uh . . . well, dear, reindeer eventually shed their antlers," Mom said.

"That's it," Grandma said, "Rudolph has shed . . ."

"We're going to keep Rudolph in our shed?" I asked. "Won't it be dark in there? His nose doesn't look bright enough to see by."

The calf began to shake its head, and the other antlers fell off.

Grandma had just explained that reindeer shed their horns as they grow.

"Rudolph is growing fast!" I said.

Mom said I later told my little friends that I knew all about animal sounds.

"Dogs bark, cats meow, and reindeer moo," I said.

I WANTED to stay longer that night at Opryland, but after almost three hours, I had to get back to the Opry House for my second show. I walked back to the dressing room that is used by each week's different guest performers. While I'd been away, someone had taken cardboard and made a sign with my name on it and hung it over the door. They drew a happy face beside it.

"There it is," said my daddy, "your name on a dressing room at the Grand Ole Opry."

I knew who'd made the sign.

$\mathcal{I}$ HEARD her before I saw her. A tile floor on a wide aisle runs between the dressing rooms backstage at the Opry House. You can hear footsteps real well.

"I want to meet you," she said, walking through my open door. I wondered who had come in without even saying hello. I turned, and my stare locked with the eyes of my daddy's favorite singer of all time. Her eyes were blue and clear, like mountain pools. Her hair was high and looked kinda messy. But each hair was in place because it was stiff with spray. Her stage suit sparkled with jewels and rhinestones. It glowed, but not as much as her shining face.

I had heard my parents play her records since before I could remember. I had seen her on television many times, mostly on shows about the Grand Ole Opry in the days before I was born. But I saw her on some of the cable channels, too. Her presence was something to see—and to feel. She could not have had such a glow on her face unless she had joy in her heart. I felt as if I had known her all of my life and wanted to know her for the rest of it.

I can't tell her name. I eventually promised I wouldn't. Keeping her identity a secret was the only condition she imposed before agreeing to let me share her story.

She knows about the lesson she taught me. She told me a forty-six-year-old story in the space of a day, and it changed my life forever.

"I'll bet you're glad to be in here and off of that travelin' contraption you call a bus," she said with a smile.

"You must have been reading my diary," I joked. "The bus isn't so bad. I'd rather be on it than in the finest jail in Tennessee."

(At that time I was traveling with ten others inside an old used bus. Most of the room was taken up by our instruments and other stuff, and the space left over for us was about the size of a walk-in closet.)

"I'll tell you somethin' else," she said. "I'll bet you're 'bout ready to move to Nashville."

"What makes you say that?" I asked.

"I can see it in your face," she replied.

"You can? How so?"

"Because I once saw that there same look on me," she said.

Her smile didn't fall, but suddenly seemed forced. I haven't lived long enough to know everything and know I never will. But I know pain when I see it.

I suddenly hoped my enthusiasm wouldn't come off as being disrespectful. I felt like this American music legend was reliving a part of her career through me.

I was glad to let her. I knew that others before me had shared my dream. I wasn't its owner, just its current caretaker.

I was dreaming of what I wanted to do, and she was dreaming of what she had done. Our roaming minds were drawing us into a quick friendship.

"As long as you're goin' to be spendin' so much time in Nashville, you ought to let me show it to you," she said.

I wasn't sure what she meant. I felt myself staring blankly.

"There's more to Nashville than the Grand Ole Opry and neon signs," she said. "This city has a pulse and a soul, and you need to feel it if you're goin' to fit in with the musicians that'll be playin' on your records. They've got the Nashville mentality, and you need to get it, too."

"Well," I paused, "I'm going to my record company office tomorrow, and we'll probably drop by a music publishing company or two."

"Honey," she said, "that's the last thing I'm talkin' about. Real country music is sung from the heart and written from the street. When our songwriters and musicians want inspiration, they don't go to no front offices to get it.

"There's some places in this city where the tourists

don't go because they cain't get in. There's other places they don't go 'cause they wouldn't want to. Them's the places I needs to take you."

I was at a loss. Was this legend offering to take *me* on a personal tour of Nashville? I didn't want to seem dumb, but neither did I want to seem ungrateful.

"Well, uh," I said, "what will we do—go in your car?"

"No," she said, "we'll walk."

"Walk? How can we walk? I mean, you're so famous. You can't go out in public, can you?"

It was the wrong question.

"Me?" she said. "Nobody's bothered me for years. The stargazers who come to Nashville weren't born when my career was hot. They's no way most of 'em would recognize me. The fans who do know me is too old to care about seein' me or too old to travel to Nashville."

She laughed, but somehow didn't seem amused.

"No, honey," she went on, "you're the one they'll want to see. So I'll tell you how to avoid attention. Just do what I say.

"Wear loose clothes," she directed. "I suggest a pair of bib overalls. Them things is back in style for you kids, anyhow. Forget them stage clothes that show your cute figure. And definitely get a baseball cap with a long bill that you can pull down low. Put your hair in a ponytail and pull it through that there hole it the back of the cap. Don't wear no makeup and wear the largest sunglasses you can find. Do all of that and you can go anywhere in this town. Baseball caps has been around long before recorded music, and I used to use that trick in my day. The tourists is so busy lookin' for the way they expect stars to look, they overlook the way they actually do. Ain't that a hoot?"

"I know lots of girl singers who claim they use that trick and can walk into any Wal-Mart in the nation without nobody knowin' them," I said. "They don't recognize them without their big hair and thick makeup."

We giggled some more, and then it was time for me to go onstage: It was probably fifty yards from my dressing room through the corridors to the wings of the sprawling Opry stage. The legend walked every step with me. Sometimes I had to halt to sign an autograph or when somebody else in the cast or crew approached. She always stopped, too.

No one spoke to her, but many people talked to me. I wanted them to be more attentive to her. They treated her as if she were invisible. I was uncomfortable and felt like I was getting an undue amount of attention in the presence of a flesh-and-blood living institution. But I guess it was because I was the new kid on the block. These backstage workers had visited with her hundreds of times. Many had been in her home. They had seen her recently, even though she rarely performed anymore. People said that for the past few years she had mostly hung around backstage at the Opry and kinda talked to anyone who'd talk to her. The younger performers—and they were all younger than she was—obviously took her for granted.

It all made me feel a little sad.

No matter how many times people stopped me, she never left my side. She never fell behind, never stepped ahead. She was always by my right hand.

I relished having her there, especially when photographers snapped our pictures.

"I love being photographed with you," I said. "Thank you so much."

"Honey, do you know how many times I walked this here aisle?" she said. "Do you know how long it's been since anyone took my picture? They're shootin' you. They don't even know I'm here."

Due to all the interruptions, it probably took us ten minutes to reach the stage curtains.

"And now, ladies and gentlemen . . . !" the announcer said.

"I know where you're stayin'," she whispered. "I'll come by your room in the mornin' at ten o'clock."

"Miss Anna Lee!" the announcer thundered.

I stepped from the darkness and let my eyes adjust for a second or two to the blinding spotlight. I'd learned how to do that early in my young career. I walked the few feet that seemed like a mile from the curtains to the Opry's center stage, all the while nodding my thank-you to audience members on and off the platform.

Giant Christmas trees sat on each side of the stage. They were so tall, I wondered how they had been brought inside. I felt so tiny next to them. My eyes rose to the balcony and to its tinsel that hung in loops almost to the people on the first floor.

Nashville sure knew how to decorate, I thought.

"I'd better be thinking about what I'm doing," I said to myself. So I focused, but not before I turned around.

I'd never been escorted by a legend before, much less one I'd left in the wings. I felt kinda rude about that. I wanted to wave at her.

I could feel her support. But when I turned to watch her watch me, she was gone. She had somehow gotten through maybe a hundred people crowding backstage and was nowhere to be seen.

I almost forgot the opening line to my song.

Chapter Two

𝒯HE BASEBALL cap was the final touch of the disguise. The New York Yankees had just won the World Series, and I wore their emblem. No one would ever suspect anyone in country music to be a New York fan. And I put on baggy bib overalls with straps, like painters wear. I let one strap dangle. I looked in the mirror and was convinced no one would know me.

The clock in my hotel room rolled over to 2 P.M. She was obviously going to be a little late. I thought the same thing at 2:30 P.M. And our original appointment had been for 10 A.M. She had postponed that at perhaps 10:30.

I was struggling to get my ponytail back through the hole in my cap when the telephone rang. Finally!

But it was Grandpa Luther calling from Leesburg.

I could feel the desperation in his voice before I could hear what he was saying.

"Anna Lee, honey," he said, "your Grandma Teeden has had another bad spell."

"Grandpa Luther," I said, "is she all right?"

"Not this time, honey, not this time. I tried to call your mama and daddy there in the hotel, but they're not in their room."

My aging grandma had been suffering from stomach pains for a few months. My parents and I had urged Grandpa Luther to take her to the hospital at Jackson, but he had given in to her stubborn insistence that she be taken only to their family doctor, old Dr. Hyatt.

He was the one who had delivered Grandma Teeden.

Sixty-five years later, he had prescribed strong antacids for her pain that repeatedly came back—and was worse each time it did. He also had tried to get Grandma Teeden to go to a hospital or clinic at Jackson. He told her she needed X rays he couldn't take because he had no machine. He explained that she needed blood tests, but he had no access to a laboratory.

"Teresa," he told her, "I'm an old man whose time in medicine has long since come and gone. The state wouldn't let me practice if I wanted to, not out of this place. Why, I'd get in big trouble if the state board even knew I was seeing you. You go on up to Jackson and let these young doctors heal you. I don't have much more than penicillin around this old place, and even that's so old it's probably not potent."

His "office" was in fact the parlor of his daintily trimmed Victorian house. Set in a magnolia grove, it had been in his family's homestead for more than a century and was a little Mississippi landmark. As a girl, I had loved to hear him spin tales about his granddaddy's medical practice and how his most common remedy was larghum. He had said that during his grandfather's day, medicine was more superstition than science.

But he was good for the treatment of sniffles and could set a broken bone with gooey plaster and gauze. He also had an overall "potion" he invented himself that he administered more than any other medicine. It required no prescription. He gave it for everything from high blood pressure to arthritis. It must have been effective. Mom said lots of folks took it when they weren't even sick.

His services had been good enough for Grandma Teeden's mama and daddy and her seven brothers and sisters. She wasn't about to turn over her health to today's young doctors. She called them "whippersnappers with thermometers." She insisted they all had medical degrees from out-of-state colleges. That, to her, made them foreigners.

I asked Grandma Teeden once where Dr. Hyatt went to college. She said she didn't know. I asked her if I could ask him, and she said no, because to ask a doctor such a question would be disrespectful.

She bragged on Dr. Hyatt simply by saying he showed his care for his patients by his willingness to make house calls. I don't remember him ever coming to her house, except when her mare was in foal. He delivered the colt.

I thought it was unfair for Grandma Teeden to be sick anytime, especially at Christmas.

I remembered another time when I was small and how she had dressed as Santa Claus, then walked the short distance from her house to mine. It was Christmas morning. She wore the complete outfit and tried to speak in a low voice. That hurt her throat, and her "ho-ho" eventually became constant coughing. She had a snow-white beard. She spent the morning patiently passing out presents to my folks and me, and I'm told I was speechless. After she had gone, my mom asked me what I thought about our visitor.

"How did Grandma Teeden grow cotton on her cheeks?" I asked.

Mom changed the subject.

✳ ✳ ✳

"ANNA LEE, are you listenin'?" Grandpa Luther said.

I marveled at how many memories I had processed in the few seconds since he had last spoken. Funny how we harbor fear for the future and fondness for the past when our loved ones are suffering.

"Yes, Grandpa Luther," I said, "of course I'm listening. I was just thinking about what to do."

"Well, honey, you won't believe that I'm callin' you from a phone in Jackson," he said. "Your grandma finally gave in and came to a real hospital."

"How on earth did you get her to go?" I asked.

"I didn't," he said. "The ambulance driver did."

"Ambulance driver?"

"This spell was the worst one by far," he said. "Her pain bent her over double this time. She's been livin' with pain for the past few months, but this mornin' she got out of bed and just doubled over. I tried to lay her on her back, but all she did was scream. I called the county seat and got an ambulance, with her yellin' at me the whole time not to do that."

"Well then," I said, my voice rising, "what's the matter with her?"

"Don't know yet, honey," he almost whispered. "The doctors has started her on a battery of tests, as they call it. And they have an X-ray machine here, too. They said they'd know somethin' for sure by daylight.

"Anna Lee honey, your Grandma Teeden wants you to come home. You'll be here soon, won't you?"

I didn't answer him.

She had had these spells before, and I had been there to see her through each. I had never had a second thought about taking time off from school or canceling a paying engagement at one of the small nightclubs that I'd played in rural Texas with my dad after we moved there from Mississippi.

Each time Dad and I had rushed home, Grandma Teeden had seemed to recover in a matter of days— sometimes less. Dr. Hyatt would just give her a stronger batch of his potion. Wouldn't this time be like the others? I knew that no one is immortal; that was the rule. But there are supposed to be exceptions to every rule, and this exception had a name: Grandma Teeden. I couldn't imagine her staying sick for very long.

"Grandpa Luther," I said, stammering. "Is it really best for me to come all the way to Jackson? I mean, I don't know if I can do that from Nashville on a moment's notice."

"But Anna Lee—" he started to say, and I cut him off.

"Grandpa Luther, I hope you take this the right way, but I need to stay here for some really important meetings tomorrow. Tomorrow will be the most important day of my life.

"If Grandma Teeden is finally in a real hospital, she's going to have some real doctor bills," I went on, surprised at how rapidly I was coming up with excuses. "Somebody is going to have to pay all those bills, and I want to be the one. I'm of more use to her here in Nashville than I would be standing around the hospital."

There was a long silence.

"Anna Lee, honey," he finally said, "these young doctors think she has cancer in her intestines. They won't know till they get back their test results. If she has cancer, they're goin' to make her take a bunch of liquids that'll purge her system, and then they'll operate in two or three days."

"Oh great," I said. "Well, I didn't mean great, I meant I'll have two or three days to get there if they decide to operate."

"Honey, I only know what these doctors has told me," he went on, almost pleading. "They told me there were a good chance they could remove all of the cancer, but that she could have a heart attack on the operatin' table 'cause of her age and weak heart. These here doctors has determined that your Grandma Teeden has a mighty weak heart that they say might not withstand all the carvin' on her innards. They say she needs a bypass, and that they want to do one if she makes it through the cancer surgery. I never heard doctors talk so blunt. Why, old Doc Hyatt would never tell nobody that their loved one might die on an operatin' table. You reckon they know what they're doin'?"

I would have smiled at his childish question had the situation not been so serious.

"Grandpa Luther," I said, "I want to know everything that happens. But until we know if she's going to need surgery and until I can firm up the business that will let me pay for it, I really think I should stay here."

Again, a long silence.

"Grandpa Luther, are you there?" I asked.

"Pray for her, honey," he finally said weakly. And then he hung up.

I stood there with the telephone receiver held firmly against my chest. Had I done the right thing? Grandma Teeden would have plenty of family members at her bedside. She had only one family member who could finance the prolonged medical attention she might need. I had big money coming in at the end of the year and had no plans for any of it except to buy a big bus on time payments. I needed to be in meetings tomorrow, the results of which would pay for her treatment in the future. That was all there was to it. I had convinced myself.

"So I shouldn't feel any guilt," I said out loud. "Like it or not, I'm doing the right thing."

I slowly put the telephone receiver in its place. It instantly rang again.

$\mathcal{T}$HE CLOCK said 2:43 P.M.

"Sorry I'm late, honey," said the voice of the veteran star who I'd forgotten all about. "Meet me out front," she said. "I'm in a black Cadillac."

And then she hung up.

I fixed my cap, put on sunglasses the size of saucers, and walked quickly to the elevator. It was too slow, so I trotted down the three flights of stairs. I walked unnoticed through the crowded hotel lobby.

I had difficulty spotting the black Cadillac. It was so old that the color had faded to gray. One fender was badly dented, and there were scores of spots on the passenger door where it had been banged by other doors. Each of the spots had rusted. It was like the car had metallic measles.

I pulled hard on the heavy old door and remembered how my dad had bragged about the sturdiness of old cars. I slid onto the front seat, turned her way, and saw immediately that she was wearing the same gaudy outfit she'd worn the night before.

"How could anyone *not* notice her?" I thought to myself. "How far would she go to get attention?" I silently prayed that somebody would recognize her during our outing, remembering what a big star she'd been.

The floorboard was covered with discarded magazines, Styrofoam coffee cups, and other litter. Most of the paper was from candy or fast-food wrappings. Cellophane crackled under my feet. The debris was a mat so thick that I had trouble determining the color of the torn carpet.

She offered me a hamburger from a greasy sack, and I was hungry enough to accept. The french fries were cold, and the cola was warm.

"Ready to go, honey?" she asked.

She also wore sunglasses and for an instant, sunlight shone directly into her lenses. I was looking through my colored lenses into hers. Two sets of dark lenses failed to filter the light in her eye. I had seen that same glint so many times in the eyes of Grandma Teeden.

But the entertainer was not as radiant as she had been backstage. My daddy said she was flamboyant, and I looked up the word. I thought her flamboyance had faded. Yet somehow she still wore with dignity the years that had worn her out. Her struggle to be pretty made her spirit beautiful.

I recalled my dad telling me about seeing her name at the bottom of a marquee in Las Vegas, a city where years earlier she had been a headline attraction.

The sign had enormous letters announcing its star attraction and then in tiny letters said: FREE, IN OUR LOUNGE, _____.

"They had her playing amid the cigarette girls and the expense account crowd," Dad complained. "She's forgotten more than most of those people will ever know about show business. That sign broke my heart."

She and I drove through bumper-to-bumper traffic to a Nashville neighborhood she called Lower Broadway. We passed the Ryman Auditorium, and she parked in front of the Ernest Tubb Record Shop, for years the home of the *Midnight Jamboree*. My parents had told me how the show went on the air promptly at the stroke of twelve, right after the Grand Ole Opry. It was carried on WSM-AM, which for decades was a 50,000-watt, clear-channel station. On a clear night, before the days of FM radio, the *Midnight Jamboree* could almost be heard from coast to coast.

"I sung in that there place many a time," she said.

I looked upward at the spinning marquee of the likeness of Ernest, a country legend whose career flourished from the 1940s through the 1970s. He made a lot of money in Hollywood and was one of the first country stars to do so. I heard a television report that said he died broke, two years after I was born. I had been told there was no headstone for his grave. I wished I hadn't thought about that.

"They'd better never take that old sign down," she said. "That's the biggest thing we have to remember Ernest by."

We got out of the car in front of a parking meter. She walked away without depositing a coin. For a second I wondered if she had twenty-five cents and felt ashamed for having had the thought. I reached into my pocket for a quarter.

"Forget it, honey," she said. She opened the car door and threw the hamburger wrapper onto the floor, where it joined the other litter.

"You think anybody's goin' to tow that car 'cause there ain't no money in the meter? The towin' fee would cost more than the car's worth."

Her laughter was strong and sweet and was music itself. It came from deep inside. As we walked, she went into a couple of sidewalk cafés for coffee refills holding the same Styrofoam cup.

We walked along Lower Broadway past the places that sat next to all the popular new restaurants and nightspots that she explained had opened since 1988, the year of country music's most recent popularity explosion. She told me I knew a lot of dates. I said that boys knew sports statistics, and I know facts and stuff about country music.

The Christmastime tourists were shoulder-to-shoulder. They were literally bumping into a legend and didn't know it.

"After the Opry left the Ryman," she said, "this here neighborhood was taken over by a pretty rough bunch of people. But after country music's popularity came back, the city saw to it that things got cleaned up right fine."

I saw the Hard Rock Cafe, Planet Hollywood, and other national restaurant chains. Merchants had their wares in front of open stores and yelled at people walking by. The neighborhood was Nashville's Times Square.

Perhaps it had to do with the season, but for some reason none of the fast-talking hawkers seemed like hustlers. They were aggressive but polite. Many of the open stores played Christmas music that leaked onto the street. The weather was cool, brisk enough to be stimulating.

"And from Fort Payne, Alabama, Merry Christmas tonight" came the recorded lyrics from the band Alabama. A few more steps, another storefront, and "God Rest Ye Merry Gentlemen" was playing.

I loved being in one more American city that celebrated Christmas before Thanksgiving.

"I wish I knew what to get my dad for Christmas," I said. (I had earlier told my parents I was going Christmas shopping for them, and I was. That's why they let me out without a chaperone.)

I was astonished at her reply.

"Give your dad what Jesus gave His dad," she said. "That's all parents really want from someone your age, anyhow."

"What on earth did she mean?" I wondered. "And what did she know about Jesus and His dad? And what did Jesus give His dad, anyway?"

We turned left on Second Avenue, and I saw many of the electric signs that I had seen on national television. I melted into the casually dressed crowd as if I were camouflaged. She was as bright as walking neon, but she had been right. No one stopped her. The tourists were young enough to be her children's children. They were people who liked modern country music because it was what everyone listened to. They didn't know—or care—about its history. These were the fans who bought a song because others had bought it first.

I could have told them her name, and they would have asked, "Who?" I could have sung the lyrics to any one of her classics, and they wouldn't have known a word.

I remembered reading where broadcaster Ralph Emery said that the most difficult thing he saw in show business was not an artist's struggle to climb to the top. It was a star's struggle to come down with dignity.

My eyes were peeled for gifts for each of my parents and grandparents. I wasn't a very good shopper. And anyway, my mom and dad and my grandma and grandpa were happy with what they had and didn't really want much else.

We passed a furniture store, where a television set wrapped in Christmas paper with a bow on top was playing. Only the screen was visible. It was set to a cable channel that was showing an old *Lawrence Welk Show* rerun. I had watched all of those reruns when I was a little girl sitting in Grandma Teeden's lap. The two of us sank deeply into her worn-out "television chair," an old piece of living room furniture that was threadbare. She often said she was going to throw it away when it wore out.

I chuckled to myself when I remembered how she never did throw out that old television chair, no matter how worn it got. We'd just sit there and watch Lawrence Welk on Grandma's old black-and-white TV.

I couldn't understand why that funny-talking man kept poking at the bubbles floating around him with a giant pick. Why did he want to burst them?

Seemed like she knew every song from every show and said she had seen them in their "first run" before I was born. I didn't understand how the television once ran, but now just stood there, scratched and with a fuzzy picture in the corner. When she was out of the room, I used to kick it to try to make it run again. During those years, I even thought Lawrence Welk was a little man inside a box with lots of little friends.

Maybe I could buy my grandparents and my parents new televisions, I thought.

Naw, I decided, they didn't need new televisions. That was out.

I tried hard to think of anything I'd ever heard any of

my people say they wanted. The only thing I recalled was when Grandma Teeden told Grandpa Luther that she would like new dentures for Christmas. I was about six, and that was the same year Grandma Teeden and Grandpa Luther celebrated their fiftieth wedding anniversary.

My parents' and my grandparents' friends from the church came for a big celebration. It was so special that Grandma even turned off Lawrence Welk. There was ice cream and cake, and sentimental gifts like an electric mixer and a curved knife for cleaning fish. I thought it was wonderful. Grandpa loved to fish, and Grandma had always hand-cranked her mixer.

When the party was over, I asked my grandma and grandpa if I could spend the night with them. My young mind didn't even consider they might want to be by themselves.

Mom said no before either grandparent could answer.

"Oh, let her stay," Grandma Teeden said. "She's the best thing we've got to show from this marriage. I cain't think of nobody I'd rather have."

Mom still said no, but I kept begging, Grandma kept insisting, and so Mom finally gave in. Not only did I stay with them, I slept in their bed. I just climbed right in between them as I had done all of my short life. I thought nothing about it. That's where I always slept at Grandma's house.

I now know Grandma thought I was asleep when she began whispering to Grandpa about their wedding that had happened a half century earlier.

"Luther," she said, "fifty years ago tonight, as we lay in bed, you held my hand."

Grandpa's arm reached across me, and he picked up her hand.

"Luther," she whispered again, "fifty years ago tonight, you kissed me."

Grandpa struggled to sit up, leaned across me, and kissed Grandma quickly on the cheek. He lay back down with force, as if sitting up had worn him out.

"Luther," she said again, "fifty years ago tonight, you bit me on the ear."

Grandpa got up and began stumbling around in the dark, mumbling all the time.

" 'Bit me on the ear, bit me on the ear,' " he kept muttering, repeating what Grandma had said.

"What are you doing out of bed?" Grandma asked him.

"What do you think?" he said. "I'm looking for my teeth."

*M*Y NEW friend and I crossed Nashville's Lower Broadway and started west. We passed more open stores and eventually walked past Tootsie's Orchid Lounge, the hangout of every star and songwriter in the country music industry from the 1930s through the 1974 move of the Opry. It is situated across the alley from the Ryman, and the Opry stars used to make the short walk from the stage's wings to the bar for a few drinks between performances.

We paused in front of the old Tootsie's building. Its paint was peeling, and above the front door hung a fading sketch of Hank Williams, Sr. We didn't go inside; I wasn't allowed.

"If you was old enough," she said, "I'd take you in there and show you where Hank Williams and Johnny Cash wrote their names on the wall. I could show you autographs from Johnny Horton, Roger Miller, Webb Pierce, Faron Young . . .

"Do you know who I'm talkin' about?" she asked.

"Yes," I smiled. "I grew up on their records. My mom and dad played their songs all of the time. I even do a Hank Williams song on my show. I love traditional country music."

"But Hank's been dead for nigh on fifty years," she said. "And you're so young."

I didn't answer. On the bustling street, I sang Hank's lines at a level that only she could hear.

Did you hear that lonesome whippoorwill?
He sounds too blue to fly

That means he's lost the will to live
I'm so lonesome I could cry

She smiled widely and her eyes again sparkled magically. There was no way to mistake her pleasure.

It seemed most of Tootsie's customers were older. I was sure that one or two would come out, recognize her, and want an autograph. I prayed a second time that that would happen—and quickly. She was supposedly showing me the town.

"Hey!" a drunk man said, colliding with her.

"Thank goodness," I thought, "someone finally recognized her."

"Didn't you used to be Kitty Wells?" he said.

"No, I didn't!" she snapped. "Kitty Wells used to be Kitty Wells, and she still is. Didn't you used to be sober?"

This gal could bite.

"I'm sorry he bumped into you" was all I could think of to say.

"He didn't see me," she said. "He didn't see me."

We crossed Fourth Avenue and continued walking westward up an incline. We headed south across Broadway at Eighth Street. She kept telling me which direction we were going. The day's temperature was at its daytime high, yet the air retained its wonderful seasonal chill. Traffic was thick, but motorists were forgiving in the way they only are at Christmastime. And in the air was the sound of country Christmas songs. It was so special.

I had been caught up in the spell and hadn't noticed that we had wandered slightly out of the tourist district.

Suddenly she stopped in her tracks and spun on her heels.

"Now look back down there, honey," she said.

My eyes raised eastward into the neighborhood we had just left and into the towering Bell South Building, the tallest building in Tennessee. Closer to us stood the new Municipal Arena, the grand opening of which was scheduled soon with a Christmas concert by Amy Grant and Vince Gill. Faith Hill and Tim McGraw were scheduled for the arena's second concert on New Year's Eve. Little did I know then that I'd perform there in February with Alan Jackson.

The arena covered an entire city block, and I could smell its newness in the late-afternoon breeze.

"That there place holds twenty thousand people and cost $145 million to build," she said. "Now look directly in front of you."

I wondered why she had stressed the numbers.

I had been staring so hard into the distance that I hadn't noticed the one-story structure a few feet before me. It was a rescue mission.

I wondered about the placement of the modern building so close to a home for the down-and-out. Before I could think much more, a man held out his palm to her.

"At last," I thought, "an old fan has recognized a former great. Or is he holding out his hand to me?"

It didn't matter. All he seemed to want was a handout. In the literal shadow of hundreds of millions of dollars' worth of new construction, a battered man begged for pennies.

From inside the mission I could hear old voices singing "Silent Night." And the woman who hadn't fed the parking meter opened her purse. She handed the man silver. I noticed how hard she dug to find the pieces. He didn't say anything. He just looked at his open hand and then seemed to stare right through her.

A tired-looking woman rang a bell for the Salvation Army, and people passing by shoved bills into a pot in front of the ragged men coming out of the mission. Then something happened that I'll never forget.

A man in a topcoat and tie was in a hurry and thrust his bill into the pot without stopping. The bill went in a little bit, then the wind whipped it onto the street.

I followed it with my eyes into the dirty hands of a man wearing clothes that were more like rags. Almost nothing fit. He picked up that bill, ten dollars, and smashed it into his fist.

I looked at my friend and she looked at me. We both

wondered what would happen. That bill wasn't meant for him; it was meant for the poor.

"But who is more poor than him?" I thought.

He slowly began to walk toward the Salvation Army woman and her bell, and when he got a step or two from her, he stopped. She instantly stopped her ringing. People were used to its sound and looked in her direction when it became silent.

The bell ringer, the street person, my new friend, and I were the only ones who knew the man had money intended for the collection pot. The old guy stared hard at the bell ringer, then slowly put the hand clutching the money inside his pants. They were jeans and the only clothes that kinda fit. With his other hand, he tried to pull open his tight front pocket, so he could force his hand with the money deeper inside.

Still, no one had spoken.

I could see the outline of his fist reach the bottom of his pocket. I saw it open, and I saw his hand stirring. Then, still moving slowly and without a word, he brought the hand with the money out of his pocket.

It held that wrinkled ten-dollar bill—and some pennies. He put it all into the collection pot. He had reached into his pocket not to keep the money he'd found, but to add the little he owned.

"Bless you, young man!" the bell ringer said. She was almost shouting.

He looked down the sidewalk. He still had not looked at any of the rest of us by the time he lost himself in the holiday crowd.

"Right down there is that famous guitar shop," she said after the man moved on. "You know, the one on the television commercial where they say, 'Bring your Visa 'cause they don't take American Express.'" I marveled at how much of the stuff around me I had seen on television.

"I got one more stop on our little walkin' tour," she said.

She hand-led me into, of all places, the bus station next to the mission. It was jammed with holiday travelers.

"Why would I want to see a bus station as a part of my walking tour of Nashville?" I almost said out loud. "Didn't I spend enough time on a bus of my own?"

Had I not respected the lady and her legacy, I would have suggested we return to the car.

"This place is full of people goin' home for Thanksgiving who might not come back till after New Year's—if they come back at all," she said. "Many have got no place to go and nobody to go with. Some of these ol' boys look a little rough, but they won't hurt you. Life has beaten too much out of 'em for that. They don't have enough energy to be mean."

I was amazed at how the entire place smelled like burning shortening. The kitchen was twenty yards away, yet could be smelled the moment the front door was opened. I noticed so many people traveling with their belongings in paper sacks. I could see their clothes through the holes in the bags. It was heartbreaking.

"You won't see no designer luggage here, honey," she said. The wind had blown her hairdo. Its spray had kept it from getting mussed; it had simply gotten bigger. It was like hair filled with helium.

She stopped talking only long enough to fetch a donut from her purse. It left powdered sugar on her lip.

She offered me a donut, but I'd had enough food. So she ate mine.

Old men sat in chairs attached to coin-operated televisions. Most of the televisions had snow on the screens, as twenty-five cents' worth of viewing time had expired. But the men didn't move. They had paid for a warm place to sit and sleep.

She showed me a picture on the wall of George Jones's house in Brentwood, a Nashville suburb. There were words under the picture. The sign didn't mention that George had moved four years earlier. I knew because I had seen his new mansion in many of the country music magazines I had read. Another picture and text described Tammy Wynette's house. I also knew that she had moved out years ago.

"The place is really up-to-date, ain't it, honey?" she said, laughing.

"Come this way," she said and led me through giant doors.

I stood on the docks where the buses arrived and departed. Before long, a roaring coach pulled into a stall, and its passengers wearily strolled off. Except for those carrying guitars.

They had a bounce in their step and a confident air. It was obvious they were coming to Nashville to try their luck in the music business. Hope was in their every move.

Their enthusiasm was somehow uplifting to me, and I told her so. She smiled, but only halfway, and into the distance.

"Wait a few minutes," she said. "That same bus will be pulling out soon."

The dock was elevated and whipped by the wind, whose edge sharpened as darkness began to fall on the city.

"Why on earth," I wondered, "are we standing outside in this cold to stare at a bus? And how come she knows this place so well? Is she reduced to hanging out here at the bus station?"

I was making a silent joke, but it was as if she could read my thoughts.

"I come here often to remind me of something," she said. "I had my day in the limelight. Listen."

A voice over the loudspeaker announced the final call for loading. We had stood there and simply watched people we'd never met get on a bus whose destination we didn't know.

"They'll come," she said. "They always come, and they're always the last to board."

Three men stepped through the giant doors. Two held guitars. Their heads were bowed, their shoulders stooped, their steps slow.

"Remember them guys a few minutes ago, the ones who was just arrivin' in Nashville?" she said. "You could tell they was full of faith as they prepared to try their luck in country music. Well, the guys you're seein' now has tried and failed. Their futures is behind 'em. See the one without a guitar? I'll bet we could find it at that shop on the television commercial. That place buys used guitars, and I'll bet that guy had to sell his to buy his ticket home.

"These here kids saved a long time to get here, and it was hard," she went on. "But it was harder to save enough to get out. You see, honey, you can see the Grand Ole Opry on Friday and Saturday nights. What you're seein' now is the Opry that goes on three hundred and sixty-five days a year. And you'll see an encore of this here show with just about every bus that comes in and goes out."

She was right. The men getting on the bus, as opposed to those who had earlier gotten off, wore failure like a uniform. They dragged their feet to the bus that would take them where they were going because they could no longer afford to stay here. The sight was sad, and I didn't want to look. But I somehow couldn't turn away. I wanted to rush up to each of my brothers in music, and tell them to come back, and wish them better luck next time. But it was obvious these men didn't want to be encouraged—or even noticed.

"How did you know about this?" I asked. I instantly wanted to withdraw the question and felt my throat tighten.

"I rode one of these here buses myself once," she said. "Course, it was a much older model, and it didn't leave from this station. This station wasn't even built then. But in all the changes I've seen in Nashville, this scene has remained the same, this same ol' picture of men with spirits broken by shattered dreams.

"Shall we?" she asked.

She extended a hand that held two bus tickets.

"What in the world . . . ?" I said.

"We're not goin' far, only about thirty to forty-five minutes down the interstate. We'll catch another ride right back. It's the holidays, and buses run often. We should be home in plenty of time for supper."

"I don't want to ride a bus," I said. "Can't we take your car?"

"We could, but it'll be better if we take a bus. Trust

me. You could *hear* what I'm going to tell you in my car. But you'll *feel* the story on a bus."

I stared at her in disbelief. A light snow was beginning to fall, and her stiff hair held the flakes firmly. Darkness crept over the blinking downtown that was her backdrop. The bus driver revved the engine and looked through the windshield directly at us, as if to say now or never.

Without another word, she turned her back to me and walked up the two stairs into the aisle of the bus. I stood motionless for a moment and was astonished when I felt myself follow her.

Chapter Three

I RODE the bus for one block and wanted off. I planned to get out at the first red light. I had silently rehearsed what I would say.

"I know there is something you want to show me, but can't you just tell me?" I'd say. "I really have a busy day tomorrow, and I'll be glad to pay you back for the bus tickets. You can tell me about what we were going to see while we walk back to the car."

I turned to speak, but stopped after noticing her glasses. She still wore the dark lenses, although nightfall was now everywhere. The bus's tinted windows made the darkness even blacker. Why did she want dark glasses?

The glow of a Christmas ornament fell at just the right angle, and I could see her tears. I hurt for her. There was no way I could beg out of the trip now. And so I stayed on board. Frost was beginning to form on the windows, and that made it cozy inside. I pulled my collar high and nuzzled deeper into my seat.

I looked out the window at the car tops beneath me. They glowed with the reflection of Christmas lights. Those reflections would soon be covered by snow.

I realized I had been told how long I'd be gone, but not where I was going. And so I asked.

"This thing stops in Jackson, Tennessee," she said. "It's about a hundred and thirty miles down the road."

"I thought you said we'd only be gone thirty to forty minutes," I said, forcing cheerfulness. "But you want to show me something in Jackson, Tennessee?"

"No, no!" she almost shouted. "Ain't nothing in Jackson except people who wished they lived in Nashville. We'll get off before that."

Get off? I wondered what she meant, and that annoyed me. She owed me an explanation. And I wondered if every state in the South had a city named Jackson.

Hadn't I agreed to come on this ridiculous trip? Weren't we on our way? There was no way I could get off, so didn't she think it was time to reveal the mystery?

But I didn't pose any of those questions. My feelings for her were still a mixture of respect and pity. I was glad I had told my parents I was going Christmas shopping, but I realized that if I was gone too long, they would worry. I needed to get back to the hotel reasonably soon. In my eyes, I was independent. In their eyes, I was fourteen.

The bus pulled onto Interstate 40 west toward Memphis. Nashville was in the rearview mirror in no time.

She pulled a pickle—an unwrapped pickle—from her purse. Juice dribbled down her chin. I could hardly think about eating when she offered me one. I said no, so she ate both.

The purr of the highway beneath us was the only thing similar to my own coach. A couple of passengers were snoring. If I had had a blanket, I could have, too. So much space and peace at highway speed made me feel secure.

"Moving is the closest thing to being free," sang Tom T. Hall. I knew what he meant. This bus didn't feel like a prison but like a protector, shielding me from all the pressures that would be waiting when it stopped. For an instant, I didn't want it to. Snuggled into the seat that seemed to wrap itself around me, I felt safe.

I was thinking about Grandma Teeden as we passed the Tennessee farmhouses, sparkling with Christmas lights, one after another outside my window. Many sat far from the highway, deep into darkened fields. Other houses were tucked into thick woods, and the blinking lights along their roofs peeked cheerfully through the trees. I couldn't see the houses, just the lights that framed them. It was like seeing sparkling Tinkertoys. Their glow seemed to make it darker inside the bus, and I wondered if it was as dark inside Grandma Teeden's hospital room. I tried to take comfort in the fact that Grandpa Luther was with her.

"He *is* with her," I told myself.

"Boy, this bus is really comfortable," I said to my friend and fallen star. "I'm already glad we took it and not your car."

"Yes," she said, "it's comfortable. Bus travel has a negative public image in some circles. Why, most people don't even realize there's a restroom on this thing or a loudspeaker for the driver to talk to the passengers like a pilot on a jet. Course, buses wasn't always this way. They wasn't always this way at all."

I could tell she wanted me to ask what she meant, but I didn't want to talk about buses. I had wanted to ask her a hundred questions about her life and career, but thought I'd seem nosy. Yet I had agreed to come on this trip, so she owed me a few answers, I figured. I really wanted to hear her recite her memories. I knew this woman would be a great storyteller.

She had mentioned the Ernest Tubb Record Shop earlier, so I asked her if she had ever worked with Ernest outside that place.

"Only at the Grand Ole Opry," she said. "He had that same thing about clocks that Marty Robbins had. You know about Marty Robbins, don't you? 'Cause he's dead, too."

I told her I did and that I had sung "Don't Worry About Me" when I was on television's *Star Search* as a little girl.

"Marty always played the Opry from eleven-thirty until midnight," she said. "At the stroke of twelve, the show was supposed to be over, and the house lights was supposed to come up. There was a giant clock on the stage for the audience to see. At about five minutes to twelve, Marty would take his guitar handle and stick it in the air on the big hand on that clock. He'd push the hand back fifteen minutes, and the show would run overtime. Them folks in the audience got more show than they paid for, and they loved it. Why, they clapped and hollered and carried on something fierce. I never seen no man that loved to sing more than Marty did, and he pulled that stunt every Saturday night for years.

"There we was, live on a radio show that was supposed to end at midnight. Grant Turner, the old announcer— course, he's dead, too—but anyhow he'd come on the microphone and sign the show off the air with the music still playin'. Once in a while he'd tell the radio listeners why Marty was still singin', and Marty'd get letters from folks all over the nation thankin' him for actin' up that way. They thought it was funny, and they liked to see somebody buck authority.

"Course, Ernest wasn't so timid about the clock," she continued. "You know he pulled out a pistol and shot an Opry clock right off the wall one time in the fifties 'cause he thought his show had been cut short. Seems old Ernest had been into the joy juice—if you know what I mean, child. Right in front of a packed house, he starts firin' away. Women and kids was screamin' and people was duckin' under them bench seats we had at the old Ryman Auditorium. Ernest just turned around from the clock and started singin' again. Acted like he hadn't done nothin' wrong.

"Well, that deal made the papers all across the country," she said. "After that, every time somebody dropped an instrument or anything happened that sent a 'boom' over the Opry radio network, folks wrote in to ask if Ernest had shot up the place again."

She told me about the night Hank Williams made his debut on the Grand Ole Opry and the famous story about his five encores.

"But that ain't nary a bit true, honey," she said. "It was six."

She remembered the one and only time Elvis Presley

ever played the Opry and how his feelings were hurt because he sang a new kind of music called rock 'n' roll that the Opry managers didn't understand.

"He was just a scared kid from Mississippi, your home state," she said. "He went to shakin' and carryin' on, and when he was finished, this here Opry big shot told him not to come back. Told him to go someplace else to play his jungle music. I know I saw tears come into his eyes. I know I did."

"But what about the road?" I asked. "Wasn't it hard for a single girl in the forties and fifties to travel with all-male bands?"

"You don't know the half of it," she said. "The men thought that women who sung country music was supposed to be ladies, and ladies was supposed to be at home. They'd do anything they could to make me cry and give up and go back."

She told me the men in the various bands she worked with would secretly turn the tuning knobs on her guitar seconds before she walked onstage. She said she'd hit her first chord and then have to stop the show during her first song to tune her instrument.

"I was paying them guys, but they didn't like me having hit records that they thought men singers should have. They only worked for me when they couldn't get work for men singers. Every time I came off the road, half of my band would hire out to any man singer needing musicians, and I'd have to throw together a whole new group in time for my next tour."

She told me that some of the rowdy musicians once replaced her shampoo with glue. She rubbed it into her hair and had to have much of it cut off to get rid of the glue.

"And that was back in the days when women didn't wear short hair," she said. "I couldn't work for several months while my hair was growin' out."

"I think that's awful," I said. "I don't know how you took it."

"Who says I did?" she said.

I should have known this spirited woman didn't get her spunk overnight.

"You're not old enough to remember real shavin' soap," she said. "Men today use soap in aerosol cans, but years ago they used to put a round bar of soap in a mug. They ran hot water through a brush and rubbed the brush on the soap to make a lather. They smeared that lather on their beard and shaved it off with a razor. That's how barbers did it, too."

"Okay," I said. "So what?"

"Nobody in my band was gonna admit to puttin' glue in my shampoo bottle," she said. "So I came up with an idea to get even. Back in the fifties, there was a soap factory on the Cumberland River that runs through Nashville. I went down there and bought a big block of lye soap and hired a man to cut it into circles that would fit inside shavin' mugs.

"Do you know what lye soap is?" she asked.

I told her I didn't.

"Well, it's about the strongest soap there is," she said. "People used to use it to clean grease off of car motors or put it on a wire brush to take rust off of steel. I put five pieces of lye soap into five shavin' mugs for my band members. Them boys lathered up and shaved, and their faces was broke out in about thirty minutes. See, after soaking their beards in lye, their razors took off the top layer or two of skin when they shaved. None of them could understand how they'd all come down with a rash at the same time. We was onstage and half of them was a-missin' the beat. They'd play a lick, then scratch their face. They liked to have rubbed their chins raw—and didn't have no idea why. I told 'em what I'd done to 'em after we got back to Nashville, and everybody in the whole band quit. I told 'em I was sorry and wanted to give 'em severance pay. I gave each of them another bar of lye, and one of 'em threw it at me.

" 'You ought to be makin' babies instead of music!' " he said and stomped off.

"It was hard on girl singers in country music in them days," she said.

"I laugh about it today," she went on. "Course, back

then, when I was a young girl, I used to go into them old hotel rooms and cry out loud about the way the men musicians and show promoters treated me. But I never let 'em see me cry. And you know what, I miss it more than anything in the world. That's a fact, honey, that's a fact. Enjoy it while you can, even if it makes you cry. 'Cause they'll come a day when you'll miss the show life, and you'll cry 'cause there's nothin' left to cry about.

"Show business was my tar baby," she said, "and it'll be yours, too. Once you pick it up, you cain't ever let it go. Then someday it'll let you go, and nothin' else you touch will stick with you the way it did. It's a mighty sad thing."

$\mathcal{S}$HE REACHED to turn on an overhead light inside the bus. Its pin beam shone into her lap. Then she turned on the one above my own seat.

She opened her purse, and I thought I saw a photograph of a cross—a white cross. There was nothing else in the picture, just that cross. I decided I hadn't gotten a good look.

"Here, Anna Lee," she said and handed me a wrinkled and yellowed newspaper. "This here's old and brittle, so open it careful now."

"What's this?" I said.

"Part of the reason I brought you out here," she

replied. Our eyes remained locked until I looked at the clipping.

Carefully, I unfolded the creases until a full newspaper page lay on my lap. A circle had been drawn around the date at the top: November 24, 1950.

"That was the day after Thanksgivin' Day," she said, although I hadn't asked.

BLINDING SNOW SWEEPS AREA, MERCURY TUMBLES read the front-page headline.

"I'm told it was Tennessee's worst snowstorm of the century," she said, "but I don't know for sure. But I can tell you there ain't been none that bad in these here parts since."

I've only lived in Texas and Mississippi, where any snowfall is rare and one inch is almost considered an avalanche. Schools and businesses close, which is kinda neat because all the kids and some of their parents stay home to play in the snow. I've seen television news reports about those enormous snowfalls in the North. But those storms seem as far away from my world as the Yukon. I can't imagine anything like that, any more than Northerners can imagine picking Florida oranges in December.

On the last Friday in November 1950, the temperature fell thirty-nine degrees in nine hours in Nashville, the newspaper said. And it kept falling. By 2 A.M. the next day, the temperature was one degree above zero, one of the coldest readings ever, according to the report. The temperature had tumbled sixty-two degrees in twenty-four hours.

I thought of how Grandma Teeden hated cold weather and how we'd snuggle up to each other in front of her old black-and-white TV whenever we'd get one of our cold spells back in Mississippi.

Those conditions in 1950 were the result of a blast of cold air from Kansas that nobody forecast. I remember studying about weather forecasting in science class and how it wasn't too reliable until weathermen became meteorologists. I still really don't know what a meteorologist is, even though I called a television station to find out.

The result of Tennessee's cold air in 1950 was the middle South's version of an "arctic onslaught." Those are the big words the newspaper used. It not only took Tennessee people by surprise, it eventually took many lives, the newspaper said.

The next part of that story really fascinated me. It said that automobile wrecks were so frequent in Nashville that an important man who worked for the city just disconnected all traffic lights. It really said that. The city man thought he'd keep drivers from trying to stop their cars, which would end all the skidding. Instead, drivers were going head-on through the lights from four directions at once. I wonder if the man who disconnected the traffic lights lost his job.

My daddy has always said that people do desperate things in desperate situations, and I guess that's true. The people in Tennessee a half century ago were desperate and panic-stricken. My friend said they "lost their logic to Mother Nature's fury." I suspect she had heard a smart person say that.

"Why are you showing me this newspaper?" I asked her.

"You see that part where it talks about the city buses runnin' as much as five hours behind schedule?" she asked. "Well, the highway buses was in even worse shape. The bus lines eventually stopped them from travelin', but some of the coaches that was on the road when the blizzard began was stranded. There wasn't no interstate highways in Tennessee then and no snow removal equipment. There wasn't no snow fences and still ain't to this day.

"So out here," she continued, motioning to the countryside, "the wind whipped the snow so hard that the windshield looked like milk on the bus I was ridin'. And you cain't see nothin' through milk."

"You were on a bus during that storm?" I asked. She went right on talking.

"We had been out of town for about an hour—too long to turn back. And a driver cain't turn a bus around on no two-lane road. The bus is too wide. He has to drive all the way to the depot or find a side road. See, this here road we're on—it's got grass between the four lanes.

Them old two-lane highways only had a stripe between lanes. There wasn't no room to turn around.

"I was goin' to a show somewhere in Arkansas. And it just kept snowin' and blowin'. Back in Nashville, it stopped before it reached ten inches. See there? It says so in the newspaper. The whole city was paralyzed.

"But out here, on what used to be a state route, the snow was whipped into drifts as deep as six feet on the sides of the road. You know why? 'Cause the land was bare pasture. There wasn't no crops to stop the driftin'. Our driver couldn't even see his rearview mirror on the outside of the bus 'cause the snow was comin' so hard. I remember he told a passenger to sit next to the back window and holler if a car was comin' up from the rear. But that passenger couldn't see nothin', neither.

"I've been in plenty of snowstorms, but that was my one and only blizzard. There wasn't no time for nary a farmer to get his livestock out of the fields. Do you know that some of the pigs smothered? They was actually buried alive in drifts. Some of the cattle got stuck in high snow and like to have starved to death before they was pulled out in a few days. See, the farmers had to wait for some thawin' before they could get their tractors in the fields to rescue the cows."

I couldn't imagine anything like that. I would have

thought she was exaggerating if I hadn't held the newspaper in my hand.

"A lot of the bus passengers panicked that day and began to beg the driver to stop," she went on. "But he couldn't. Somebody would have driven right into the back of us. He was drivin' as slow as that bus would go without its engine dyin' out, and he was drivin' blind. He couldn't see the highway, and he couldn't see the ditch. Finally we hit it head-on and drove right down the slope to the bottom. The road was up above us. By the next day, the drifts in that there ditch were almost as high as the bus windows. Honey, we was stuck."

By now, I was hypnotized by her story. I waited a long time before I spoke.

"You mean you were in that ditch all night?" I asked.

"All night and then some," she said. "Yes, sir, all night and then some."

She pulled off her sunglasses and stared out the dark window, not really looking at anything. Her speech slowed the way it does when adults are thinking hard about what they're going to say next. This woman had been singing stories for all of her life. She knew how to communicate. The fact that what she was telling me was true added to the fascination. I was clinging to every word. I hoped I wouldn't interrupt her again. But I couldn't resist.

"I can't wait to hear more," I said. "Is this why you brought me on this ride, to tell me this story?"

Without glasses, the annoyance was visible in her eyes. It almost outshone the light.

"No," she said softly. "I brought you out here to show you somethin'. You'll see it soon enough. But you need to hear what I'm tellin' you before you do."

She turned from me and didn't speak for at least a full minute. I knew I was going to hear the rest of her story, but I wondered if I'd get to hear it on this trip.

She suddenly dug deeply into her bag and retrieved a Moon Pie. I began to wonder if she was carrying a purse or a refrigerator with a strap. The candy's wrapper was so old it stuck to the cracked chocolate. This woman was a certified junk-food junkie. She took a hefty bite and, with a full mouth, settled back to tell more of her story.

"Now," she finally said, "the bus hit the drift and the ditch and people screamed. Remember, those passengers weren't even accustomed to heavy snowfall, let alone to gettin' stuck in the stuff. Two or three jumped out of their seats. The driver didn't know what to do, neither. He kept changin' gears with the shift on the floor and gunnin' the engine. But the tires just kept on a-spinnin', and the inside of the bus filled with fumes. Everybody was coughin' and carryin' on somethin' awful.

"I believe today's buses has two-way radios on 'em.

What's that term—'radio-dispatched'? Course, today's buses would be on an interstate highway after a snow-plow had done gone down it. But back then, our driver couldn't call nobody. He didn't have no radio.

"Now here's one of the worst parts. Those old buses used to run what were called 'local routes.' That meant they'd stop at every little town and even at places in between. People could stand by the road in their yards with a suitcase and flag down the bus. The driver would pick 'em up where they stood, and he'd drop 'em off wherever they wanted. The Nashville to Memphis route had a stop at every little town on the way. That meant that part of the route included blacktop roads. And we had been on a blacktop road off the old State Highway 100 between Lyles and Wrigley when we went into the ditch. You ever hear of them places? I don't think nobody but God had in 1950.

"Well, honey, I guess we would've kept warm if the driver hadn't turned off the engine, but he did what he had to do. I didn't know nothin' about carbon monoxide in those days, but I do now. The engine's exhaust couldn't go out a pipe 'cause the pipe was under the snow. It had nowhere to go 'cept right up into the bus, and it would've killed us all.

"We would've fallen to sleep and woke up dead," she laughed. It was her first laughter since leaving Nashville. Her joke broke the spell of her storytelling.

"I can laugh about it now, honey," she said. "I can laugh about it now.

"Really, if the driver could've run the heater, we would've been warm and fed," she said. "In those days, it took a long time to go anywhere on a bus, and people brought along lunches. Two or three had picnic baskets on that bus. But even so, we still run out of food.

"The engine hadn't been off but thirty minutes before it got cold, and inside an hour it was like bein' in an icebox. People got out of their seats and began to walk up and down the aisle. The driver had a flashlight, and that was our only illumination. People would yell at him, asking the time, and he'd shine that light on his pocket watch. The rest of us couldn't even see our watches.

"We would've all froze to death, except that people dressed warmer in those days on them drafty ol' buses. But even our heavy coats didn't keep people from thinkin' they was goin' to die. Your mind plays tricks on you, honey, when you're just sittin' in your misery, waitin' and prayin' that somebody will rescue you.

"It's funny who'll keep their cool and who won't, pardon the pun. The first passenger to lose his was a big ol' burly guy who had a rugged face like raw meat. I can still hear him to this day. 'We're gonna to freeze to death! We're gonna freeze to death!' he started yelling. You know that big ol' feller was actually cryin' while he was a-screamin'?

"By midnight, we had paired off, two to a seat, and we hugged. We hugged each other tight. We was sharin' our body heat, you see? They was no danger of nobody fallin' asleep—it was too cold. We just sat there shiverin' and clingin' to one another.

"Do you know that not one car came by all night? Not one car was out there on that ol' blacktop road. Course, if there had been one, it probably would've been stuck, too. And he wouldn't have seen us nohow 'cause we was down in the ditch, and the road was up higher than a man's head.

"The snow blowed off them pastures into our ditch all night. By daylight, like I said, it was nearly piled plumb to the bus windows. You thought such things only happened in the movies, didn't you? After the snow finally stopped fallin', it still kept blowin' and blowin' and blowin'. It hit the side of that bus as hard as sand out of a cannon. People held their ears to keep 'em warm and to lock out that awful noise.

"People used to carry thermos bottles with 'em on trips in them days, and lots of folks had brought coffee. Our sandwiches froze, and we had a hard time chewin' off the bites. We'd have to hold the bites in our mouths to let them kinda thaw before we could swallow. A man leaned out a window and shoveled a big pile of snow into the bus with his arms. We'd walk to the pile and scoop up handfuls of snow, let it melt in our mouths, then swallow it for drinking water.

"Makes me hungry just talkin' about it," she said and pulled a sack of fried pork rinds from that bottomless purse. "We'd been in the ditch all night by then," she continued, still munching, with crumbs on her chin.

"And still nobody came?" I asked. I reached for a pork rind, so she wouldn't interrupt the drama by offering one. "What about the people who were expecting you at your destinations. Didn't they send a search party?"

"Yes, honey," she said, "they finally did, and that was one of the worst parts of all. You're too young to know about road graders. They were big, long things that weren't no more than a steel frame and a giant blade that was as wide as the road. The blade sat at an angle and pushed anything in its path off to the side. I haven't seen one in years.

"Well, remember how I told you our ditch was so deep? We feared we couldn't be seen from the road, and that's exactly what happened. The road grader came by twice after the snow stopped. It pushed snow off the road, into the ditch, on top of the bus! The grader driver didn't know he was burying us alive.

"There were two or three cars that braved the road after the grader went down it. We'd hear a faraway engine and start jumpin' up and down, screamin' in the bus. But that grader and those cars would just drive by on the road above us. They couldn't see us. The snow was piled against the door, so we couldn't get out to climb the ditch to the road."

I could resist no longer.

"Why didn't somebody go for help?" I asked.

She looked at me as if I were insane.

"Somebody tried to do more than that, honey. This one man said he'd walk until he found help, and another man gave him a second coat and a second pair of gloves. He was goin' to be our savior, and I remember he said he'd go 'cause he was single and didn't have no family. After that many hours on that stranded bus, we really thought he was our hero. I even kissed him. Everybody was thankin' him and turnin' loose of each other just long enough to pat him on the back.

"Those old bus doors used to have a joint down the middle. When they were opened, part of them stuck outside, while part of them came inside," she explained. She folded her hands to illustrate.

"Well, the driver still couldn't get the door to open against the piled snow. So we picked the window above the smallest drift. It might've been five feet or so. Some men on the bus helped this guy out the window, feet first. The rest of us put our faces against the other windows to watch. This guy wasn't too tall, and I remember he kept sinkin' and sinkin' into the drift. By the time his feet touched solid ground, he was in snow up to his chin. He couldn't move to go nowhere. He had a terrible time just gettin' his arms raised. The men took his hands and pulled him back up through the window into the bus. That old snow had us trapped. There weren't no escapin' that bus.

"I think that was the most terrifyin' time of all. And that's the word I mean, honey, terrifyin'. You see, it had taken us all night to finally accept that nobody might not come for us way out there. But now we realized we couldn't go to fetch nobody, neither. Think about that.

"Even in this day and time, you read about people on snowmobiles or cross-country skiers freezin' to death in some backwoods where it snows so fast and blows so hard they can't get back. Them people sometimes has cellular telephones and still can't get rescued. They wasn't no cellular phones in 1950, honey. And they wasn't no rescuers to call between Lyles and Wrigley."

I hadn't spoken for several minutes. When I finally did, I couldn't believe what I asked.

"How did people go to the bathroom?" I said.

She laughed for the second time, and this time it was from her belly. She looked around the warm bus that was taking us through the Tennessee night, as if to relish its safety.

"Honey, people get real immodest when they think they're in trouble, especially when they think they're gonna die. By the second night, the men even stopped openin' the windows 'cause they didn't want to let in the cold. People just went to the same place in the back of the bus, and nobody looked when they did. It was so cold in there that things froze almost instantly—if you know what I mean.

"I guess that nightfall on the second day was the worst time. People was exhausted and couldn't stand to see the sun set on our isolation. Everybody had pretty much run out of food, and somehow things seem more hopeless when you cain't see. It was dark as pitch by five o'clock, and that same ol' boy who had panicked earlier totally lost his mind. Two or three others had been hysterical by then, and they also started screamin' that we was gonna die. Meanwhile, people kept walkin' and huggin' themselves, tryin' to stay warm. We had kinda developed a traffic flow, you know? That first hysterical guy ran into all of them and was knocking people down.

"Well, honey, I told him to get ahold of himself. He said somethin' smart, and from out of nowhere came a fist. Knocked the guy smooth out to shut him up. We had to shake him awake 'cause he might have froze to death if he stayed out.

"We was feelin' our most doomed when somebody got the idea of burnin' the bus seats to get warm," she went on. "We wondered why we hadn't thought of it earlier. The driver had a wrench, and we took the seats out of the floor. We cut the vinyl with a pocketknife and pulled out the stuffin'. It was dry and caught fire real quick. We had to open one window, and one guy used cardboard to fan the smoke outside. It didn't work all that good, and most of us coughed and breathed a lot of smoke. But a live fire inside that tin bus heated things up real nice. We must've tore out a half dozen of those seats and burned 'em up. Kept us from freezin' alive. You ever see homeless people do that around fires inside barrels up North? They stand right out in the wind, but inside that bus, we got warm as toast. I still don't know why we didn't think of it earlier. Course, earlier, we didn't think we'd be out there for so long."

I had not heard about many natural disasters in my short life and had never met anyone who'd lived through one. This woman had told the story so well that I felt I'd been through it with her. I hate to use the word "entertaining," but her incredible story would have been entertainment to anyone.

When I first started singing, my daddy told me that people always are drawn to people who entertain them. Perhaps that's why I was drawn to her—that and the fact that she was the former idol of millions who was giving her attention only to me. I had known her less than twenty-four hours, but she'd become like a lifelong friend.

No one can hurt you like your friends. So I was crushed when I saw it.

I'd heard about drug abuse in school, but had never

known anybody who used illegal drugs. In fact, I don't think I'd ever known anybody who'd known anybody who'd used illegal drugs. She opened her purse, dug beneath that picture of the cross and the junk-food sacks, and pulled out a kit.

"Hope you don't have a weak stomach, honey," she said. "I suppose I could go to the bathroom to do this, but my hand will be more steady if I keep my seat."

She pulled out a syringe with a needle.

"I'm just goin' to give myself a little injection," she said. "Then I'll be feelin' right fine. Right fine."

I turned toward the window, watched the dark landscape pass, and kinda tried to watch out of the corner of my eye. But I didn't really want to see.

And I didn't want her to see me cry.

Chapter Four

"*I* HOPE I didn't make you uncomfortable," she said. "I'm sorry you had to look away. It embarrasses me, too, when I do that around folks. Don't have to do it in front of folks that often, though."

I couldn't believe my ears. Legend or not, I'd seen enough. I was tempted to ask the driver to let me off right there.

"You mean you've done that in front of strangers?" I asked.

"When I've had to," she said.

"Aren't you afraid of getting arrested and going to jail?" I said.

Her face was blank. Then she exploded into laughter. Two people a couple of rows ahead turned in their seats.

She tried to talk, but her laughter wouldn't let her.

"What did you think that was, honey? Dope?" she asked.

I felt myself blushing. Blood seemed to be pounding in my face.

"Yes," I said. "What else could it be?"

"It was insulin!"

"Oh," I said. We rode for perhaps the distance of a city block, her laughing and me blushing, before I asked, "What's insulin?"

"I'm a diabetic!" she said. "I take insulin. Diabetics are people with too much blood sugar. They take insulin to regulate the sugar. Haven't you ever heard of a diabetic?"

"Yes," I said, "I've heard of one, but I never thought I'd meet one."

More howling.

"Honey, we're all around you," she said. "There are millions of diabetics in this country. People used to die from diabetes until doctors learned about insulin. For years now, us diabetics has injected insulin into our blood with syringes every day, some of us two and three times a day. Then we go on with our normal lives."

I was so relieved. I asked her if she would do it again and promised to watch closely this time.

More laughter.

"We don't just inject whenever we take a notion," she said. "We have to do it on schedule. It was time for my shot, that's all. I won't need another until mornin'. Look, let me put this in plain talk. I'm what's called an insulin-dependent diabetic. If I get my insulin, I'm fine. If I don't, I go into insulin shock. Leave me in shock long enough, and I die. But that's never happened, cain't you tell?"

Just as suddenly as she had begun, she ceased to laugh. Her face was serious, then sad, then distant.

I felt I had said the wrong thing and told her so.

"It's nothin' you said," she said. "It's somethin' I'm about to say. It won't be long now."

With that she rose from her seat and grabbed the tops of each seat to hold her balance as she walked toward the front of the moving bus.

"Come on, honey," she said, looking down at me. "This is where we get off. You tell the driver to stop."

"What?" I said.

"Don't worry," she said. "We have a ride."

"We have a what?" I wondered. And I also wondered why she didn't tell the driver herself.

I obeyed and drew a mysterious stare from the driver when I told him we wanted to get off in the middle of nowhere.

He looked around to see who was with me, looked blankly at me again, and then shrugged and started to stop the bus.

"Come on," she said. "Come on."

She turned and started for the door. Following her simply because I was asked was getting to be a habit. And a tiresome one.

Had she forgotten that I had to be in Nashville tomorrow for the most important meetings of my career? Didn't she realize that I wanted to be rested for them? I was out here at personal sacrifice, and I began to wonder if she appreciated that.

"And what about Grandma Teeden?" I wondered. I wished I hadn't gotten so far from a telephone. I felt guilty about not knowing about Grandma Teeden's situation. I felt anger toward my legendary friend, then felt guilty about that. How could I please everybody? There were so many places I needed to be. Why was I fooling around in a bus in the Tennessee countryside?

The coach came to a complete stop and the brakes breathed hard, as I'd heard them do so many times on my own bus. I heard passengers muttering as we stepped off the bus, into the night and onto the asphalt shoulder. The door closed with a bang behind us. Fumes boiled around us as the bus roared back into motion. A car's engine got louder as it approached, then got softer as it drove into the distance on the far lane of the interstate.

Then all was quiet. The two of us were alone on a black and isolated highway, and she had planned the whole thing.

I was nearly blinded as I was hit squarely in the face by headlights. In the darkness, I couldn't see the car, but it was her black Cadillac, parked a few feet away. It was hidden behind high beams turned directly into my eyes.

"There's our ride!" she said.

We began walking toward the lights. We headed to the passenger's side of the car and stepped off the road's hard surface into weeds. She opened the door. I had no idea who was in the dark interior.

A single, dim light shone inside. I instantly recognized the driver as the man outside the Nashville bus station, the one who had extended his hand. I thought she had given him coins; instead, she'd probably handed him her car keys.

"Anna Lee, this is Carl," she said. "Carl, this is Anna Lee."

I bent at my waist to peek inside.

Carl said nothing except "You get in."

Carl seemed bewildered to be picking us up, but I dismissed it as the behavior of someone I didn't know.

He had just gotten the car up to highway speed when he slowed for a sign that read 48 SOUTH. We turned onto a paved road. A sign said LYLES 5 MILES.

We rode in silence until she said with a chuckle, "What

did you think of Lyles?" The town was so tiny and the night so dark that I had completely missed it. We turned onto State Highway 100 west and I saw a sign for Wrigley. By then I knew where we were going. I wondered why she'd want to visit the site of that bus accident forty-six years later and wondered even more why she'd want me to see it.

"What will there be to see?" I thought to myself.

The headlights shone on pavement that was bumpy from the tar stripes across it. I had seen cracked roads like this in rural Mississippi, but this was my first off-the-interstate experience in Tennessee. There were no utility lights, no billboards, and nothing else was visible along the highway. Had Carl turned off the headlights, we would have been swallowed by blackness.

For the first time since meeting this woman, I felt afraid. The concrete before us was the only sign of civilization. I felt isolated and alone in the middle of nowhere.

"All right," she said to him, "it's right about here. Should be any time now."

The dark country night exploded into daylight. A cross that was perhaps ten feet tall and six feet wide was suddenly as bright as noon in July, not twenty feet from the pavement's edge. Carl stopped in the middle of the road, even with the glowing cross. My eyes were still adjusting, and I couldn't look directly into the beam.

"What do you think, honey?" she roared. "Did you think you was meetin' your Maker when that light came on?

"Ain't it a dandy? It's made of a steel frame covered with weatherproof plastic. You can see right through the plastic. It's, what's that word . . . ?"

"Transparent," Carl said.

"Yeah, that's what it is, transparent. The insides of the cross is filled with twelve-volt bulbs. Twelve volts is the size of car headlights, you know. We got twenty-four bulbs goin' up the cross and twelve across. When that lights up, you can see it for miles. Trouble is, there usually ain't nobody for miles around."

I couldn't take my eyes off the brightness. A giant, solitary cross miles from nowhere that lit up the country-side. I guess it shone for maybe a quarter of a mile in two directions. It shone on everything in that distance, which was nothing at all, except weeds.

"What is this?" I said. "How do you know about this? What makes it work way out here in this field?"

"Whoa, little missy," she said. "Not so fast. Carl helped me make this here cross," she said. "He was a welder by trade back when he worked. He welded the frame and put in all them light sockets. He wired it, too. I just plugged in the bulbs. Then he covered the cross with that transportation . . ."

"Transparent!" Carl corrected.

"Yeah, that transparent plastic," she said. "You see that utility pole?"

I could see it.

"Well, them poles is all along here, but you hadn't noticed 'em 'cause it's so dark. I went to the Hickman County rural electric service and subscribed to electricity. I got an electric meter in my name on that pole, but you cain't see it from here. Them poles carries electricity to the farmers that lives back on the dirt roads off this highway.

"The cross only lights up when somebody drives by, so that's the only time I pay for electricity," she said. "Last month, my bill was seventy-four cents!"

She howled with a laughter that came from deep within.

"What made the lights inside the cross come on?" I asked.

"Oh, that ain't nothin' but a simple motion detector switch," she said, "the kind people has on their garages. Somebody gets within fifty yards and lights come on."

Carl had not turned off the car engine. We were parked in the middle of the road, but in no danger. We could have seen approaching headlights on that flat land for a mile, maybe more.

She had left her door open and was partially illuminated by the interior light in her old Cadillac. She stepped away from the car in the direction of the cross, standing on the pavement's edge.

"Look here," she said. I stepped to her side as she flipped on a flashlight she must have taken out of the car. It shone on weeds that were between us and the cross.

"Them weeds is cattails," she said. "They grow in standin' water, and they can get taller than a man's head.

"Looks like you could just walk through those to the cross, don't it, honey?"

I nodded my head.

"Let me show you somethin'."

She picked a large rock from the gravel shoulder and tossed it into the weeds. A couple seconds of silence seemed to pass before I heard it land. The rock had fallen through the weeds onto frozen water below.

"Those short weeds is actually six or seven feet tall, but you wouldn't know it unless you fell in. They're growin' from the bottom of the ditch—the ditch our bus drove into when this was just a blacktop road. Course, them weeds ain't growin' now, 'cause the frost got 'em a few weeks ago. They're just standin' there dead. But somebody just looking at this would have no idea how deep it is, don't you know? That's why this rail's along here, 'cause you cain't tell by lookin' that there's even a ditch here, let alone how deep it is."

I hadn't noticed the rusty guardrail, whose color blended into the night.

"This rail stretches along the top of the ditch, but only where the ditch is deep," she said. "That's only about two hundred yards, or at least that's what they told me when I had the rail built. Just from lookin', you'd have no idea that twenty-eight people nearly breathed their last out here, would you now, girl?

"We'll be gone in a minute, and just as soon as our motion gets out of range, the cross's lights will go off. Don't you know this cross has scared a few people half to death when it came on way out here?"

She threw her head backward and laughed that signature laugh. Had there been a few standing structures, her howling would have echoed.

"Why did you put it out here?" I asked, knowing she intended to answer that question in her own good time. But my curiosity wouldn't wait.

"Come on, honey, get in the car," she almost whispered. "I've got one more story to tell you."

I looked at the cross through the rear window as we drove off; then suddenly, just as she had said, it went off. The highway and fields behind me were total blackness. It had truly been the only light for miles around.

※　　　※　　　※

"*I* HAD had a visitor in Nashville on November 23, 1950," she said. She spoke more slowly now than ever, as if measuring every word. "It was my dad. He'd ridden a bus all the way from Conway, Arkansas, where I was raised. I didn't have no telephone in those days, and neither did he. He'd written me three letters sayin' he'd be at my house for Thanksgivin', but I didn't answer a one of 'em."

"Why?" I asked.

She appeared to be thinking, and when she thought for a long period of time, she always seemed to eat.

Goo-Goo candy bars are a sugar staple of the South and have been a sponsor of the Grand Ole Opry for years. They are a mixture of chocolate, peanuts, and marshmallows and are in the shape of a circle about the size of a baseball.

I wasn't surprised, at this point, when she unwrapped one and talked while munching. I wasn't even surprised when she unwrapped a second.

She was riding in the front with Carl, looking out the windshield while talking to me in the back. She put her arm on the back of her seat and turned around to face me.

"When my daddy came to see me, it was after me and him hadn't spoke for a long time, and I didn't see no reason to start," she said. "See, honey, back in my day, 'nice' girls didn't go into show business. I rode the first bus I could to Nashville the day after I graduated from high school. My daddy didn't speak to me for a week before I left, and he wouldn't even see me off. My mama cried for days 'cause I was leavin' home when Daddy was mad at me. He was ashamed of his daughter going into the sinful world of show business.

"My people was real religious, and they was a young boy in our church that took a shine to me. He was gonna be a preacher, and Daddy wanted me to marry him. He wanted me to have babies and live my life right there behind that tiny church outside Conway.

"But I wanted to sing country music, not gospel songs. To make a long story short, when I left home to chase my dreams, my daddy disowned me. He said I was shamin' the family by runnin' to the 'devil's music.' He compared me to Jezebel in the Bible. The only time he contacted me was to tell me my mama had died. I got his letter the day of her funeral.

"I had them hit records in the late forties and people knew me far and wide," she said. "Lo and behold, I started gettin' them letters from Daddy, sayin' he was a-comin' to see me. You know what I thought? I thought he was comin' to ask me for money. Everybody asks you for money when your career takes off, honey. You'll find that out. Well, I was pretty big for my britches. So I didn't see my own daddy when he came to town for Thanksgivin'. I locked my door and put up a sign that said: 'Gone until someone is gone. He knows who he is.'

"I found out later that Daddy slept that night in the bus station. I guess he had a ticket to get home on, but no money for a room. He waited all day for his bus to leave and left town without ever seein' his only child. His heart must've been more broken than anyone ever described in a country song."

She choked on her words. We must have ridden a full mile before she spoke again.

"I'd took the bus on the way to my show and thought I wouldn't have to see him," she said. "I guess I didn't have no plans to see him never again.

"Did you listen to what I said a while ago about bein' diabetic and takin' insulin?" she asked.

"Of course," I said.

"Well," she paused, "that was the hardest thing of all about that bus accident. You see, I was diabetic way back then, and I was takin' insulin. I've took it all of my adult life. The day I got on the bus for my show, someone got into my purse at the bus station. They took my billfold and some other useless stuff. They also took my insulin and probably didn't even know what it was. In those days we carried it inside a little thermos in ice. We'd take it out about an hour before the injection to let it warm, then put it into a syringe. We had to sterilize the syringe with alcohol before we could use it again. I usually carried one pack of insulin and several sterilized syringes. They weren't disposable like they are today.

"That night, when the bus was in the ditch, it came time for my injection and I discovered my loss. And I became hysterical. If the cold didn't kill me, the diabetic shock would, I knew for sure.

"I began to cry and held it back as much as I could," she went on. "I didn't want to upset the other passengers. I told you some of them was already out of their minds 'cause they thought they was goin' to freeze to death. So I had my gloves over my mouth. Nobody could've heard me weepin' 'cept a mouse or a blind person. Blind people hear real good, you know.

"This old fellow with dark glasses came from the back of the bus and sat beside me. By the way he felt his way into the seat, I immediately knew he was blind.

"He asked me what was wrong, and I told him he wouldn't understand, 'cause not a lot of folks knew about diabetes and insulin in those days. But he pressed me, and I wanted to tell somebody, anyhow. It's just that I thought a blind man stranded in a blizzard had enough problems of his own without havin' to hear mine.

"But he knew everything about diabetes. He told me it had taken his sight. And he still used insulin himself, just to stay alive.

" 'I've done lost my eyes to that diabetes,' he said. 'I'll

be danged if I'll lose my life.' He smiled when he said that, and he had the sweetest spirit I'd ever seen in a man.

" 'You won't lose your life, neither, honey,' he said, ' 'cause I got enough insulin here for both of us.'

"He said he had it inside a pouch and kept the pouch in the waistline of his pants. His body heat kept the insulin from freezin'.

"That stranger was literally a lifesaver. He had a worn satchel that I guess was his only piece of luggage. Inside his bag, he said, were many empty syringes—and more insulin than he'd need before reachin' his destination.

"Well, you could have knocked me over with sheet music when he told me the amount of his dosage. Why, it was exactly the same as mine.

"Then he told me my speakin' voice was as pretty as my singin'.

" 'You know me?' I said.

" 'Oh yes, I know exactly who you are,' he said. 'In fact, you're my favorite singer. I hope someday you record a gospel album. Gospel's my favorite music.'

" 'I cain't believe you recognized me just from hearin' me talk,' I said.

" 'Well, I heard you earlier with some other passengers. Us blind folks see with our ears, and we can recognize a lot of things folks don't think we can.'

"Remember me tellin' you that me and all of them

other passengers paired off with other people to hug?" she continued. "Remember? I said that holdin' on to one another helped us share body heat a little bit. Well, I clung to that old man all night and through the next day. He had some awful sandwiches in his dirty satchel, but that was more than I had. He's the one who gave me the food earlier that I had to hold in my mouth to let thaw.

"We didn't talk a lot," she said. "We was too cold and, I guess, too afraid. So I just stared at a tiny cross that was on his satchel. It wasn't like the medical crosses that you see on Army tents. It was like the cross where Jesus died. And when the night was at its blackest, the moon shined through the bus window on that tiny cross. I stared at it for hours and knew that as long as I could see it, I was still alive. And for years I've thought about that cross. And just here lately, I put one that's the same shape—and a thousand times bigger—near the spot where I almost died. That's why Carl and I built that electrified cross back there."

"I guess the man and his medicine meant more to you than anything ever has," I said.

"That's an understatement," she said. "But I've got a little more to tell you about that man.

"I told you nobody talked much when things got really bad, but when he spoke, it was mostly about his daughter, and how much he loved her, and how he wanted to move to Nashville to live out his life next to her. I really think that talkin' about her did more to keep him alive than anything.

"I heard all about her. But I was too concerned with stayin' alive, so of course I didn't ask no questions, not even about her name or where she lived.

"The old man would get quiet for the longest time, and I'd try to peek behind his glasses to see if he'd fallen asleep. I didn't even know if blind people closed their eyes when they slept. He wore a knit cap pulled over his forehead and ears. He had long hair and a beard, not the kind that men wear today to be in fashion, but the kind that's shaggy. It was the kind men wear when they don't have no money for a barber. I eventually found out that he was so poor that his home state bought his insulin for him.

"It was time for my shot, and I hated to wake him. And I was so cold that I was afraid that I couldn't inject myself—and even more afraid that his insulin had froze.

"That's when we heard the men beatin' on the bus door."

She told me how a rescue party inside a truck had followed a road grader down the isolated highway. An airplane had searched for her bus, she said, all of the previous day, flying over its route from Nashville to Memphis. The search had begun a few hours after the bus hadn't arrived at its destination. But the bus's top had been covered by snow and was invisible from the air.

During the second day, a pilot noticed the smoke that came from the burning seats. He couldn't understand how anything could be on fire in a snowfield and flew to where he had seen the smoke, leading rescuers to the bus.

"When them rescuers pounded on the door, people began to yell and cheer like you've never heard, honey," she said, still facing me in the backseat. "It was like they was no longer cold or anything. I shook the old man to try to wake him up, but it was no use.

"I began to scream for him to take his insulin, thinkin' he'd entered insulin shock. The truth is, he'd been in shock for hours. Maybe all night and all day. You see, he hadn't had any spare insulin, like he'd told me. He'd only had enough for himself, and he'd been givin' that to me. And in that weather, he couldn't live without proper blood in his system. With his hat and beard and dark glasses and the darkness outside, I couldn't tell he was in shock. He'd been shiverin' something fierce, but I thought that was from the cold.

"The man died in my arms. I hadn't even known he was dead.

"I was hysterical when I realized he was gone, and I guess everybody thought I was screamin' 'cause I was happy about the rescuers. I tore open his bag and that's when I discovered no insulin inside. That's when I realized he'd given his own life-savin' insulin to me.

"I remember bein' so weak that the rescuers had to

carry me up the hill to their truck. I told one of 'em I was overdue for an injection, and there was a doctor with 'em. He gave me what I needed.

"After the last passenger was inside the truck, it started out behind the road grader for the main highway, which had been cleared. We was taken back to Nashville. But those people, who'd come within an inch of dyin' themselves, didn't want to ride with a dead person. So the man who had saved my life was left inside that stranded vehicle, alone in the cold and dark. The bus became his temporary tomb. The driver locked the door and twenty-seven people headed for the warmth that one man would never know.

" 'He'll be all right,' somebody said. 'This weather'll keep him froze till he can get a proper funeral.'

"I was readin' the newspaper two days later," she went on. "It ran a story about our accident and the search for us and the rescue and all of it. And it had the name of the man who'd saved my life. That name jumped off the page at me.

"The dead man was my dad.

"When I wouldn't see him in Nashville, he'd used the return part of his bus ticket to head back for Conway. I didn't know that he was by chance on the same bus as me. I don't guess it was much of a coincidence 'cause not that many people traveled in those days and not that many buses headed west out of Nashville. I hadn't seen him in so long, and he looked so different, and he had all that hair and cap and stuff on his head. And nobody told me he'd gone blind. How could I have known it was my dad?

"He probably didn't know I was on that bus till he heard me talkin'. When I'd talked to him about my diabetes, he hadn't been surprised 'cause he'd always wondered if his daughter turned out diabetic—like him.

"He probably first thought we'd be rescued in time for him to get some insulin, but when we weren't, he told me he had enough for both of us. He knew that givin' his last doses to me could kill him, but he did it anyway. The dad I'd refused to see gave his life for me."

I felt like I'd been hit with a hammer.

"You see, honey," she said, "if you have family, you have everything. After Mama died, my only family was my dad, and I turned him away. I heard you talkin' that night at the Opry about how hard things is in the rat race that's your new life. But no matter how crazy things get on that crowded old bus of yours, you're out there with your family. They'll go through anything for their daughter, and you won't really understand that until you have a daughter of your own. Whether you sleep in a comfortable bed or whether your bus is overcrowded, all of that is not important if you have your people with you. And they tell me your people are with you twenty-four hours a day.

"And do you know the greatest thing you can give your family?" the legend said. "Think about it. I do, especially at this time of year.

"That's what I meant when we was talkin' about gettin' your daddy's Christmas gift when we was downtown."

I had no idea what she meant and told her so.

"Look," I said, "I know from Sunday school that Jesus was born in a manger to parents who'd been turned away at the inn. His dad was Joseph, His mother was Mary, and Jesus became a carpenter as a young man. But I don't remember any Bible verse about what Jesus gave Joseph for any Christmas."

"Honey," she said, "you misunderstood me 'cause I don't always talk so good. When I suggested that you give your dad what Jesus gave His dad, I really meant to say Jesus' father—His heavenly father—God Himself. Give your father what Jesus gave His father—loyalty."

I was totally confused, and she could tell.

"Look," she said, "Jesus gave the ultimate loyalty. His father had commanded Him to die on a cross, and Jesus didn't have to do that. He could have called a thousand angels and removed Himself from that cross. I mean, He had turned water into wine, made the lame walk, and had even risen folks from the dead. Don't you think He could have spared His own life that day on the cross?

"But He didn't because His father had told Him to die. He was loyal to His father's wishes. If I had family today, and if any one of them asked anything of me, I'd obey. Family comes first—it's first above wealth, fame, career, success—any of those things. Family comes first. Give family the greatest gift of all. Give loyalty."

The drama of her story and the moral she attached to it were too much for me. I struggled to hold back the tears. Only then did she turn around in her seat to face the road before her.

Chapter Five

WE PULLED into Nashville with more time left in the evening than I had realized. I hadn't traveled far, but I'd heard much. That made me feel I'd been gone a long time.

Carl drove directly to my hotel.

I stepped from the backseat and stood under the awning that covers arriving guests. She rolled down her window, and I stepped back from the car to get a full view.

"Thank you so much for goin' with me," she said. "I know you thought the trip was just for me. But I hope you learned somethin' today that you'll carry with you always."

Those were my exact thoughts. Carl accelerated the engine, and the clunker rolled away from the hotel door. I saw her taillights cross the parking lot and watched them blend with other traffic leaving the hotel.

Inside, I ran past the elevator directly to the stairs, too impatient to wait. Taking the stairs two at a time, I looked at my watch and realized I'd been gone for little more than four hours. That wasn't unreasonable, and I suspected my folks thought I'd gotten caught up in my Christmas shopping.

Bursting into my folks' room, I cried, "Mom, how is Grandma Teeden?"

"She's in a lot of pain," Mom said. "Your dad just got off the telephone with Grandpa Luther. They're going to operate in the morning, but bless her heart, Grandpa Luther says she's scared to death. Poor thing has never been in a hospital in her life, much less had surgery."

The doctor, Mom said, had explained the risks to Grandma Teeden—that he might open her abdomen and find so much cancer that he would merely close her back up. She'd live out a short life on the strongest painkillers in modern medicine. Or, the doctor had told Mom, he might find that the cancer had spread to the liver, in which case an operation could be impossible. And even if he could operate, there was the matter of waiting for a donor for a transplant. The waiting list was long. If she got past each of those hurdles, there was the matter of her heart. It was weak. It might not pump blood through an open and traumatized body like Grandma Teeden was going to have at 6 A.M.

"I talked to her, baby," Mom said. "Her voice was real faint. I could hardly get any information out of her. All she wanted to do was to talk about you. She said for you to remember she loves you, no matter what happens in the morning."

I began to cry uncontrollably.

"Our first meeting tomorrow is at ten A.M.," Mom continued, changing the subject. (My comanager was going to go with Mom and me. Dad had already gone to be with his mother in Jackson.)

"We'll be getting all the dates tomorrow for your 1997 tour and finding out which big acts you'll be performing with," Mom said. "We'll have a late lunch and be at the record label to talk about your next album. We might even schedule the studio time."

"Mom, only you know how much I want this career you've helped me build," I said. "It's more important to me than anything in the world—except family. My family is my dad, my mom, Grandpa Luther, and my second mom. I want to be there when Grandma Teeden wakes up."

Neither Mom nor my manager said a word.

"Those meetings tomorrow are very important," I said, "but they can be rescheduled. If tomorrow is

Grandma Teeden's last day, there will be no rescheduling. I couldn't live with myself if something happened to her, and I wasn't there. I should have been there tonight."

My mom and my manager remained silent.

Mom looked at me through moist eyes and rose slowly from the bed. She walked directly to her purse, opened it, and pulled out her airplane ticket. Then she pulled out mine.

"I was hoping all along you'd come to this decision," Mom said. She and I were both crying when we hugged.

"I'll go to the meetings tomorrow," my manager said. "If there's any business I can't take care of tomorrow, I'll tell them we'll all come back next week. We'll tell them a family emergency got in the way and they'll understand. If they don't, we don't want to do business with them anyhow."

"I'm going to my room to pack," I said.

"Why?" Mom smiled. "All you need is in there."

She pointed to a suitcase that she had already packed for me. We were out of the hotel and in the air in less than ninety minutes.

I DON'T remember anything about the flight to Jackson except thinking about Grandma Teeden. I recalled when I'd had an infection in my leg when I was seven, and it spread to a kidney. I was given penicillin for several days before the doctors figured out I was allergic to it. I had a violent reaction and wound up staying in the hospital for three weeks.

It was my first time away from home. Mom and Dad took as much time as they could from their jobs to spend the days with me and came to the hospital every night. But they'd leave at the end of visiting hours, so they could rest for work the next day.

Then Grandma Teeden would arrive. She slept in a chair by my bed each night I was in the hospital. Sometimes I'd get scared, and she'd hold my hand and we'd sing. She always made a game out of it.

"Now Anna Lee, honey," she'd say, "we can't sing as loud as we do at home or in church 'cause we'll bother the other patients, so let's just kinda sing in whispers. Nobody will hear us but Jesus."

My young mind thought Grandma Teeden and I were doing a private recital for God.

While flying to Jackson, I thought about the time I went door-to-door selling cookies to raise money for school band uniforms. A couple of mean boys beat me up and took my money, as well as the cookies I hadn't sold.

I knew their names, just as I knew every kid in our tiny town.

I ran home, bruised and crying, and told Grandma Teeden.

Still wearing her apron, she went to the first boy's house and asked to speak to his father, a strapping man. He came to the door, and she asked if she might visit with him outside. I saw all of this from the other side of the fence, the border of his front yard.

"Your boy, Tommy, has taken all of little Anna Lee's cookie money," said Grandma Teeden. "I'd like you to get back twenty-two dollars and seventy-five cents from him, and I'll pray for Tommy."

"You're wrong, old lady," Tommy's dad said. "My son would never steal from a brat like your granddaughter."

"Oh yeah?" she thundered, her meekness gone. "Then after I pray for him, I'll whip him, right after I'm done with you!"

She jerked a string, and in one motion her apron coiled at her feet. She raised her fists, dancing like a boxer. I'll bet that man thought he had a crazy woman on his porch, and for an instant, he was right. She was crazy—and loyal.

"Now hold on here, woman!" he said and reached for his billfold. "Here's twenty-five dollars."

"I ain't got no change," she said.

"I don't want any," he yelled.

The man handed her his wallet and told her to take what she needed. She removed the bills, then handed him his own billfold.

She stomped to the man's gate and grabbed my hand in one of hers, clutching the bills in her other.

I could barely keep up as I directed her to the home of the other boy. I guess the father of the first boy had called the parents of the second. And I guess Grandma Teeden had made a believer out of all of them.

As we stepped onto the second home's front porch, I noticed an envelope held by a thumbtack to the screen door.

TERESA it said in bold letters.

"Look," I said, pointing.

She took the envelope down and tore it open.

THEM COOKIES IS STALE said a handwritten note. There were two twenties and one ten-dollar bill inside. I had "sold" all of my cookies, thanks to the collection efforts of Grandma Teeden.

On this night, while flying to be with her, I stared out the plane's window, remembering my feisty defender. I laughed out loud.

WE GOT to Jackson after midnight and decided not to go to the hospital at that hour. Mom and I slept about four hours, then made sure we were at Grandma Teeden's bedside before she woke up. It was dark outside.

I reeled when I saw her. The cancer had robbed her of

weight. The wrinkles on her face were deeper than I remembered, and her eyes sat back into her head. And someone had taken her hair down. In my entire life, I had never seen it when it was not rolled tightly into that little bun.

I crept to her side of the bed, and Dad and Mom went to the other. I could hear her breathing. Gently, I put my hand on hers.

"Don't disturb her," Dad whispered, too late. I saw the white slit at the bottom of her eyes as they slowly opened halfway.

"Anna Lee," she breathed hard. "Anna Lee."

"Hi, Grandma Teeden," I said as softly as I could without whispering. "Don't talk. Mom, Dad, and I are here with you."

"They say I have cancer, child," she said. I put my ear close to her mouth.

"I know, Grandma Teeden," I said. "Don't talk."

The room's only illumination came from light seeping in from the hallway. I was glad no one had closed the door. That would have cast her into total blackness. I wouldn't want her to wake up in that.

I'd heard adults talk about silence that was deafening. It suddenly made sense. It was suffocating, too.

I held her hand and listened again to her breathe. I didn't understand why she had a tube in her nostrils. My dad said it carried oxygen. Was she too weak to breathe? If so, how would she withstand major surgery?

Dad had explained that Grandma Teeden had not been allowed to eat for three days, as the surgeon wanted her intestines to be clear of anything that might contaminate her incision. She had been taking fluids to cleanse her bowels the entire time, and the process had left her incredibly weak. She was being fed through her veins, and in that quiet place, I could hear the dripping of nutrition into her arm. Her eyes opened for a few seconds, then closed for two or three minutes. She was struggling to wake up because I was there, and I didn't want that.

A nurse came in, and I burst out my questions.

"Why is she so tired?" I said. "Why is she so out of it?"

The nurse explained that Grandma Teeden had been given a sedative last night to help her sleep. The medicine was also intended to relax her before the general anesthetic was given that would put her into a deep sleep for hours.

"I seen you on television a whole lot here lately, baby," said Grandma Teeden. Her words startled me. "I'm so proud of you. I can't believe my little girl that sang with me so often is singin' for all of them people now."

"I know, Grandma Teeden," I said. "Don't talk."

She stared at the ceiling and I could tell she was lost in

thought. I looked at Mom, standing silently at the foot of the bed. She too had kissed Grandma Teeden and held her hand. But I don't think Grandma Teeden knew.

"It sure was nice of you to come see me, now that you're a big star and everything," she whispered. "I'll bet there's lots of other places you could be. You're moving fast, but not too fast, when you can take time to come see the ones that love you when they're sick. You're loyal to your family, child.

"Remember how we sang in my porch swing when you was little?" she said, her voice growing even fainter.

"Sure, Grandma Teeden, I remember."

"You know you're never closer to God than when you're with family," she said.

That was the second time that thought—or one very similar—had been introduced to me in less than twenty-four hours. I wondered what Grandma Teeden would think of the country legend who had said the same thing.

"Are you still close to God, Anna Lee?" she asked. "Do you still talk to Him every day? 'Cause if you're away from God, you know who moved."

I had heard her say that a thousand times. It was the motto she preached to others and the one she lived by herself. She was too weak to smile, but the mere mention of her favorite saying brought some slight motion to her face.

A nurse came in again and lifted Grandma Teeden's arm to adjust the needle penetrating it. I heard myself gasp. Flesh dangled loosely from the arm that had always been firm and full. Grandma Teeden had always been a large woman. What was happening to her?

On her farm, she worked hard and loved to eat. Grandpa Luther worked right beside her and was bone-skinny. I never heard either of them comment about the other's size.

They had been in love for more than half a century with each other's souls. She wouldn't have understood the makeup mentality that prevailed in the places where I worked.

The nurse started to pull down her covers, and I turned away. I didn't want to see how frail she'd become.

Mama later explained Grandma Teeden's dramatic weight loss. There are still some people in rural America who just won't go to a doctor unless they're nearly dead. Grandma Teeden had unknowingly been carrying cancer inside her intestines for months.

She thought it was no more than indigestion. She had been treating herself with Dr. Hyatt's potion and some home remedies that had been passed down in her family. She had read about others in the dog-eared pages of books similar to *The Farmer's Almanac*.

She had told Grandpa Luther that she had gotten to where she "couldn't hardly digest anything." The fact is, her digestive tract was being gradually consumed by the cancer.

Grandpa Luther arrived and hugged his hellos. I don't

think he spoke at all. Instead, he sat quietly in a corner and did what he always did when he was upset. He sewed. The cobbler came out in him during times of crisis. He quietly worked on a pair of lined leather gloves. He had killed a rabbit himself for the fur and had cut the pattern from a sheet of calfskin.

"These is for Teresa to wear to town when she's up and around," he said. He proudly held up the forms of fingers.

I felt warm inside, watching Grandma Teeden's soul mate tend to her the best way he knew. Had she been aware of what was going on, she would have accused him of "fussin' " over her. I'd heard their soft and loving "arguments" a thousand times while growing up. Grandpa Luther returned to his sewing. I watched closely as he sat in the dark, sewing by feel, until she spoke.

"Would you, child?" she said when she at last spoke again.

She was making no sense. Dad whispered she didn't know what she was saying. "It's the strong medicine," Dad said into my ear. "She's taken leave of her notions."

"Would you, baby?" Grandma Teeden said again. "Would you sing our song?"

I was choking with emotion and couldn't speak, much less sing.

"Sing it for me, baby," she said, her words coming in

spurts. "Sing it for your Grandma Teeden. I want to hear it one more time."

I knew she meant one *last* time.

Years ago, she had written a poem called "Who Moved?" that someone had set to music for her. She said the song came to her because people were living too fast and had "misplaced their priorities." She felt that way long before Fax machines, cable television, cellular telephones, microwave ovens, and other modern conveniences. We had later sung her tune hundreds of times. I repeated it that night, as I hoarsely and quietly began to sing.

Things that used to move us, we've moved so far above
No little things upset us, no little things like love
We've shaken all our teaching, we're close to being loose
But we're so far from God, who do we think moved?

Things they say about Him, from the manger to the man
We're not sure we really believe them, that we truly
understand
So we just don't think about Him
For faith, we gave up use
But we're so far from God, who do we think moved?

We know, we know who moved, from things that once
moved us

Holiday in Your Heart

The laughter of the children, the life: In God we trust
So now we keep us hidden, don't show what He sees
through
But we're so far from God, who do we think moved?

The good old days we can't find, can't find again somehow
Will we someday say the same thing, about days we're
living now?
Will we want to trade the future, and all that we
will find
For just a sacred second, of pure peace of mind?

For we know, we know who moved, from things that
once moved us
The laughing of the children, the life: In God
we trust
So now we keep us hidden, don't show what He sees
through
But we're so far from God, who do we think moved?
We're so far from God, and know, He knows, who
moved.

Her eyes had closed long before I stumbled through the last lines. Yet I felt she was listening. A curious glow overtook her face. It was the brightest light in the room.

Chapter Six

THE SUN wasn't up when they took Grandma Teeden from her room that day. The doctor said she'd be in surgery for about four hours, and the nurses brought her back almost to the minute.

The doctor was a nice man who looked too young to have such an important job. And I don't think of a lot of folks as being too young. He told Mom and me that he thought he'd removed all of the cancer.

"By everything I could see and feel, I got it all," he said. "I felt as much of the liver as I could, and I'm pretty satisfied that it's clear.

But I can't know for sure until the lab tests are back. They'll tell us if there is any more cancer in her body. She came through the surgery like a trouper, especially for someone her age. She might have to go through some chemotherapy as a precautionary measure, to prevent the spread if we do find more. But we're going to hope for the best."

He had cut away eleven inches of Grandma Teeden's intestines.

Dad coughed when he said that, and the doctor quickly explained that humans have more intestines than they need. He said they could give some up as easily as they could give up their tonsils.

Dad told me later he didn't believe him.

We stayed in Jackson for four days. The doctor said Grandma Teeden would be able to go home in about four more. The tests for additional cancer came back and she didn't have any, but the doctor insisted she take chemotherapy, just to be safe. Grandma Teeden pitched a fit about that.

"All of my hair will fall out," she said.

"From behind, you ain't got no hair, just a bun," said Grandpa Luther.

The painful procedures were scheduled.

Dad and I stopped by the hospital to say our goodbyes before catching our plane to Nashville. I had rehearsed exactly what I was going to say to the beloved grandma who'd been the target of my renewed priorities. My proper priorities. The words were so important to me that I had even made notes. I didn't want to forget one thought.

But Grandma Teeden was in a deep sleep when Dad and I entered her room.

"She's been knocked out all mornin'," said Grandpa Luther. "Look here at her gloves."

Dad and I marveled at his craftsmanship. He had little occasion to make things anymore in his dusty old shop. He mostly did repair work. But his dad had taught him the cobbler's craft when he was a child, and he could still put a hand stitch to leather more neatly than any machine.

The gloves were soft and supple, like Grandma Teeden's skin.

"I love them," I said, "and so will she."

"Then I hope you both like yours, too," he said.

Except for the size difference, he had made identical gloves for Mom and me. Mine fit—well, like a glove.

"But how did you know the size of my hand?" I asked.

"From years of holding it," he said.

I SAW Grandma's eyes open a few more times that day, but she was never really awake. I couldn't wait, however, for her to regain total alertness.

I had scheduled the last flight of the day to Little Rock, where I would catch a connecting flight to Nashville. On the last part of the flight, the plane was half-full and dark and somehow reminded me of that night I had taken the bus with the country legend into the Tennessee countryside. On the plane, I thought of Grandma, as I had done earlier on the bus.

I woke up much earlier than I expected the next day inside my Nashville hotel. I called my manager's room, and he said for me to meet him as soon as I was dressed. I told him to order room service and that I'd eat breakfast with my parents and him at his room.

I walked in and saw a giant calendar on his bed. My co-manager and the booking agents had done almost all of the work to lay out a 1997 tour that was geographically perfect. I was set to play every major market in every state in the nation, as well as the Canadian provinces. We were also headed to Europe. It calculated to about 125 shows, 110 cities, and half a million miles.

The routing also included the important medium markets, and I did a double take when I saw our first stop: Jackson, Mississippi.

"We'll open the year there in February," Dad said. "I figure your Grandma Teeden will be well enough to come to the show."

I was applying the final touches of my makeup for the Jackson show when somebody handed me a Federal Express package. It was from the photographer who had taken my backstage pictures on the night of my Opry debut. I couldn't wait to see the shots of my legendary friend and me and to show them to my folks. I still hadn't told them about our encounter, and I knew the pictures of my dad's favorite singer and me would really impress them and make them proud.

But she was absent in every shot. Although I had posed with her, she was not in the pictures. I was baffled.

So I told my mom and dad about her and how I had spent that afternoon and early evening with her in Nashville. I talked about our bus ride and told my dad about how her diabetic father had given up his life for her.

"I didn't mention any of this until now, because I didn't want to get into it until I could show you her pictures, too," I said. "But the photos didn't turn out. I wanted my telling the story to be special because I know she was your favorite singer, Dad."

The room became so quiet that the recorded music from the auditorium upstairs became overpowering.

"Anna Lee, honey," Dad said. "That woman you say you spent the day with, well, she died about a year ago. Seems she spent her last years with some old boy she married. They used to go to the Nashville bus station to help down-and-out songwriters and musicians. He died just a day or two after she did. Some folks think he died of nothing more than a broken heart. I don't think many folks knew—or even cared—that she had passed away. I knew it because I was her biggest fan, and somebody sent me a story out of the Nashville paper that said she was dead. The only reason her death made news was because it was so unusual. She and her husband were electrocuted while building a cross somewhere in an open field. I'm not sure anybody ever knew what on earth that was about. I don't guess anybody ever will."

I had nothing to say. I had everything to say—and I would. But not now.

It was time to go onstage.

*T*HERE WERE a lot of spotlights in our touring production. When they swirled around the footlights, they reflected in the chrome of Grandma Teeden's wheelchair, planted in the center of the front row. She was walking a little by now, but rented the chair because she thought that was the only way she could get through the crowd.

It's hard to see an audience with lights in your eyes, but her glow penetrated the blinding glare. Each time I looked at her, she was beaming at me.

My show was choreographed. The lighting and movements were all on cue, the result of weeks of rehearsal. Everything was planned.

So my band, production manager, stage manager, and

parents didn't know what to think when I stopped in the middle of my program. To tell the truth, I didn't either.

"A lot of country performers grew up singing in church," I told the crowd. "But before I sang behind a pulpit, I sang at someone's knee. She taught me that real music comes not from the throat, but from somewhere deep inside. She taught me that, no matter what the circumstances, keeping God in your soul will keep a holiday in your heart—at any time of the year. May you never lose the holiday in your heart."

I had a hard time believing that really came out of my mouth.

Then I told the audience that I wouldn't be singing for all of them today if I hadn't sung for one person many years ago. I introduced my Grandma Teeden and told the crowd she'd recently had surgery and wouldn't stand. The spotlights were focused on her. Grandma, who couldn't get to her feet, was suddenly surrounded by thousands who did. The applause was deafening.

The band was still wondering what I was going to do next. The audience couldn't hear them whispering, but I could.

I borrowed the rhythm guitarist's instrument. I pulled a stool from the wings and accompanied myself as I sang Grandma Teeden's poem turned to tune.

The auditorium was hushed.

My eyes floated to the balcony. The people at that

height were invisible in the darkness—except for her, wearing that same gaudy outfit. The lights in her eyes were like two tiny balls of fire. I had wanted to invite her to the first show on the tour, but she had come without an invitation. And my dad thought she was dead.

Carl sat beside her. I hadn't seen them since the day she and I rode the bus, and the three of us went to the cross. From the top row of the building she extended her fist, thumb pointed upward. I couldn't believe I could see her at all, much less so vividly. I glanced into the wings for my stage manager. I was going to ask him to ask the lighting guys to shine the spotlights on her. I was going to tell the crowd—and grandma—our story. I especially wanted my parents to hear it. Dead, indeed. Carl dead a day or two later, indeed.

My eyes returned to where she had been and fell on empty seats. She had disappeared as suddenly as she had appeared.

I never saw her again.

I knew that if I even tried to tell my parents about her and Carl being there, they'd just tell me that I'd been working too hard. They would probably try to cancel some of the shows we had just signed contracts to perform. So until now, her appearance at my show with Grandma Teeden has been my secret. I'll someday get my chance to thank her for coming.

But I know it won't be in this life.

The final note of my song was still bouncing around the arena as the audience maintained its deafening applause. All of the spotlights turned again to Grandma Teeden.

She put her hands on the wheels of her chair, rolled herself forward, and turned around to face the thundering audience. From the stage, I had earlier noticed the wig that covered her head, bald from chemotherapy.

And when she turned in her chair, I saw it.

Grandpa Luther had always said he could sew anything. He had woven and sewn a bun onto the back of her wig. She raised her hand to touch it, then shook it slightly. Her real bun had always shaken when she laughed.

She turned in her chair to face me again, then rolled herself backward into the row. I could see her laughter and her tears and knew she could see mine.

Then I signaled the band, and we broke into a rousing, hand-clapping gospel song. To this day, I've never felt more like singing.